Southeast Asia and the European Union

Amid the eurozone crisis, the European Union (EU) is stepping up its dialogue and engagement with and within Southeast Asia. The EU's contemporary approach towards the region emphasises the importance of open economies and common challenges of the twenty-first century. So-called non-traditional security issues have been portrayed increasingly as an avenue to share experiences and enhance cooperation between the EU and Southeast Asia. This re-orientation demands a closer look at the EU as an actor in the region.

This book is the first contemporary monograph-length discussion of the EU as a politico-security actor in Southeast Asia post-Cold War. Drawing upon the historical and institutional context and a broad range of empirical case studies, it considers the non-traditional security crises of the late 1990s and early 2000s in Southeast Asia as triggers for enhanced regional and inter-regional cooperation. In doing so, the book construes new insights into our understanding of the EU as a global actor and its normative influence in regions far away from Europe.

Providing a crisis-centric and sector-specific analysis which is much needed, the book will be of interest to scholars of Southeast Asian Politics and European Politics, as well as policy-makers.

Naila Maier-Knapp is a SEATIDE post-doctoral research fellow at the Centre for History and Economics at the University of Cambridge, UK. She takes research interest in the regional and inter-regional integrative dynamics of the EU and ASEAN, and has published widely on this.

Routledge Contemporary Southeast Asia Series

1 **Land Tenure, Conservation and Development in Southeast Asia**
   Peter Eaton

2 **The Politics of Indonesia-Malaysia Relations**
   One kin, two nations
   Joseph Chinyong Liow

3 **Governance and Civil Society in Myanmar**
   Education, health and environment
   Helen James

4 **Regionalism in Post-Suharto Indonesia**
   Edited by Maribeth Erb, Priyambudi Sulistiyanto and Carole Faucher

5 **Living with Transition in Laos**
   Market integration in Southeast Asia
   Jonathan Rigg

6 **Christianity, Islam and Nationalism in Indonesia**
   Charles E. Farhadian

7 **Violent Conflicts in Indonesia**
   Analysis, representation, resolution
   Edited by Charles A. Coppel

8 **Revolution, Reform and Regionalism in Southeast Asia**
   Cambodia, Laos and Vietnam
   Ronald Bruce St John

9 **The Politics of Tyranny in Singapore and Burma**
   Aristotle and the rhetoric of benevolent despotism
   Stephen McCarthy

10 **Ageing in Singapore**
   Service needs and the state
   Peggy Teo, Kalyani Mehta, Leng Leng Thang and Angelique Chan

11 **Security and Sustainable Development in Myanmar**
   Helen James

12 **Expressions of Cambodia**
   The politics of tradition, identity and change
   Edited by Leakthina Chau-Pech Ollier and Tim Winter

13 **Financial Fragility and Instability in Indonesia**
   Yasuyuki Matsumoto

14 **The Revival of Tradition in Indonesian Politics**
The deployment of *adat* from colonialism to indigenism
Edited by Jamie S. Davidson and David Henley

15 **Communal Violence and Democratization in Indonesia**
Small town wars
Gerry van Klinken

16 **Singapore in the Global System**
Relationship, structure and change
Peter Preston

17 **Chinese Big Business in Indonesia**
The state of the Capital
Christian Chua

18 **Ethno-religious Violence in Indonesia**
From soil to God
Chris Wilson

19 **Ethnic Politics in Burma**
States of conflict
Ashley South

20 **Democratization in Post-Suharto Indonesia**
Edited by Marco Bünte and Andreas Ufen

21 **Party Politics and Democratization in Indonesia**
Golkar in the post-Suharto era
Dirk Tomsa

22 **Community, Environment and Local Governance in Indonesia**
Locating the commonweal
Edited by Carol Warren and John F. McCarthy

23 **Rebellion and Reform in Indonesia**
Jakarta's security and autonomy policies in Aceh
Michelle Ann Miller

24 **Hadrami Arabs in Present-day Indonesia**
An Indonesia-oriented group with an Arab signature
Frode F. Jacobsen

25 **Vietnam's Political Process**
How education shapes political decision making
Casey Lucius

26 **Muslims in Singapore**
Piety, politics and policies
Kamaludeen Mohamed Nasir, Alexius A. Pereira and Bryan S. Turner

27 **Timor Leste**
Politics, history and culture
Andrea Katalin Molnar

28 **Gender and Transitional Justice**
The women of East Timor
Susan Harris Rimmer

29 **Environmental Cooperation in Southeast Asia**
ASEAN's regime for transboundary haze pollution
Paruedee Nguitragool

30 **The Theatre and the State in Singapore**
Terence Chong

31 **Ending Forced Labour in Myanmar**
Engaging a pariah regime
Richard Horsey

32 **Security, Development and Nation-Building in Timor-Leste**
A cross-sectoral assessment
Edited by Vandra Harris and Andrew Goldsmith

33 **The Politics of Religion in Indonesia**
Syncretism, orthodoxy, and religious contention in Java and Bali
Edited by Michel Picard and Remy Madinier

34 **Singapore's Ageing Population**
Managing healthcare and end of life decisions
Edited by Wing-Cheong Chan

35 **Changing Marriage Patterns in Southeast Asia**
Economic and socio-cultural dimensions
Edited by Gavin W. Jones, Terence H. Hull and Maznah Mohamad

36 **The Political Resurgence of the Military in Southeast Asia**
Conflict and leadership
Edited by Marcus Mietzner

37 **Neoliberal Morality in Singapore**
How family policies make state and society
Youyenn Teo

38 **Local Politics in Indonesia**
Pathways to power
Nankyung Choi

39 **Separatist Conflict in Indonesia**
The long-distance politics of the Acehnese diaspora
Antje Missbach

40 **Corruption and Law in Indonesia**
The unravelling of Indonesia's anti-corruption framework through law and legal process
Simon Butt

41 **Men and Masculinities in Southeast Asia**
Edited by Michele Ford and Lenore Lyons

42 **Justice and Governance in East Timor**
Indigenous approaches and the 'New Subsistence State'
Rod Nixon

43 **Population Policy and Reproduction in Singapore**
Making future citizens
Shirley Hsiao-Li Sun

44 **Labour Migration and Human Trafficking in Southeast Asia**
Critical perspectives
Michele Ford, Lenore Lyons and Willem van Schendel

45 **Singapore Malays**
Being ethnic minority and Muslim in a global city-state
Hussin Mutalib

46 **Political Change and Territoriality in Indonesia**
Provincial proliferation
Ehito Kimura

47 Southeast Asia and the Cold War
Edited by Albert Lau

48 Legal Pluralism in Indonesia
Bridging the unbridgeable
Ratno Lukito

49 Building a People-Oriented Security Community the ASEAN Way
Alan Collins

50 Parties and Parliaments in Southeast Asia
Non-partisan chambers in Indonesia, the Philippines and Thailand
Roland Rich

51 Social Activism in Southeast Asia
Edited by Michele Ford

52 Chinese Indonesians Reassessed
History, religion and belonging
Edited by Siew-Min Sai and Chang-Yau Hoon

53 Journalism and Conflict in Indonesia
From reporting violence to promoting peace
Steve Sharp

54 The Technological State in Indonesia
The co-constitution of high technology and authoritarian politics
Sulfikar Amir

55 Party Politics in Southeast Asia
Clientelism and electoral competition in Indonesia, Thailand and the Philippines
Edited by Dirk Tomsa and Andreas Ufen

56 Culture, Religion and Conflict in Muslim Southeast Asia
Negotiating tense pluralisms
Edited by Joseph Camilleri and Sven Schottmann

57 Global Indonesia
Jean Gelman Taylor

58 Cambodia and the Politics of Aesthetics
Alvin Cheng-Hin Lim

59 Adolescents in Contemporary Indonesia
Lyn Parker and Pam Nilan

60 Development and the Environment in East Timor
Authority, participation and equity
Christopher Shepherd

61 Law and Religion in Indonesia
Faith, conflict and the courts
Melissa Crouch

62 Islam in Modern Thailand
Faith, philanthropy and politics
Rajeswary Ampalavanar Brown

63 New Media and the Nation in Malaysia
Malaysianet
Susan Leong

64 **Human Trafficking in Cambodia**
Chendo Keo

65 **Islam, Politics and Youth in Malaysia**
The pop-Islamist reinvention of PAS
Dominik Mueller

66 **The Future of Singapore**
Population, society and the nature of the state
Kamaludeen Mohamed Nasir and Bryan S. Turner

67 **Southeast Asia and the European Union**
Non-traditional security crises and cooperation
Naila Maier-Knapp

68 **Rhetoric, Violence, and the Decolonization of East Timor**
David Hicks

Southeast Asia and the European Union

Non-traditional security crises and cooperation

Naila Maier-Knapp

LONDON AND NEW YORK

First published 2015 by Routledge

2 Park Square, Milton Park, Abingdon, Oxfordshire OX14 4RN
711 Third Avenue, New York, NY 10017

Routledge is an imprint of the Taylor & Francis Group, an informa business

First issued in paperback 2017

Copyright © 2015 Naila Maier-Knapp

The right of Naila Maier-Knapp to be identified as author of this work has been asserted by her in accordance with sections 77 and 78 of the Copyright, Designs and Patents Act 1988.

All rights reserved. No part of this book may be reprinted or reproduced or utilised in any form or by any electronic, mechanical, or other means, now known or hereafter invented, including photocopying and recording, or in any information storage or retrieval system, without permission in writing from the publishers.

Notice:
Product or corporate names may be trademarks or registered trademarks, and are used only for identification and explanation without intent to infringe.

British Library Cataloguing in Publication Data
A catalogue record for this book is available from the British Library

Library of Congress Cataloguing in Publication data
Maier-Knapp, Naila, author.
  Southeast Asia and the European Union : non-traditional security crises and cooperation / Naila Maier-Knapp.
    pages cm. – (Routledge contemporary Southeast Asia series ; 67)
  Includes bibliographical references and index.
  1. European Union countries–Foreign relations–Southeast Asia. 2. Southeast Asia–Foreign relations–European Union countries. 3. Security, International–European Union countries. 4. Security, International–Southeast Asia. 5. Security, International–International cooperation. 6. European Union–Security measures. I. Title.
  JZ1570.A55M35 2014
  341.242′20959–dc23
  2014006847

ISBN: 978-1-138-77637-1 (hbk)
ISBN: 978-1-138-47634-9 (pbk)

Typeset in Times New Roman
by Out of House Publishing

für Hubert und Jira

Contents

List of illustrations	xiii
Acknowledgements	xiv
List of abbreviations	xv

Introduction   1
Of crises and non-traditional security 4

1 Introduction to the analytical and historical context   12
The historical context of the ASEAN–EU relationship 15
Instruments pertinent to non-traditional security challenges 25
Conclusions 30

2 The EU and the Asian financial crisis   32
The trade and investment pledge and other initiatives 36
The role of the ASEM Finance Ministers' Meeting 41
Response within the ASEAN–EU dialogue and the ARF 45
Conclusions 49

3 The EU and the haze   51
The haze and ASEAN regional integrative dynamics 52
European assistance on the haze issue 55
The role of non-state European actors 59
Central characteristics of the EU as an actor 62
Conclusions 64

4 EU assistance in light of the Bali Bombings and avian influenza   66
The terrorist threat from the ASEAN–EU perspective 67
The case of avian influenza 76

xii *Contents*

   The EU's reaction and its initiatives 78
   Conclusions 82

5 **The Aceh Monitoring Mission**   84
   The peace process 87
   "Success has many fathers" 91
   The EU as an actor and the question of normativity 96
   Conclusions 98

6 **Non-traditional security crises since the Aceh Monitoring Mission**   100
   Summary of the EU as an actor 107
   Conclusions 117

   Conclusion   119
   The EU as an international actor in regions
      far from Europe 123
   Construing broader implications 124

   Bibliography   126
   Index   138

Illustrations

Figures

2.1 ATF 1 recipients — 37
2.2 ATF 2 recipients — 38

Tables

3.1 Forest status and burnt area — 53
3.2 Land status and burnt area — 53
3.3 Fire-related damage in US$ millions — 53
3.4 Haze-related damage in US$ millions — 53

Acknowledgements

This book has been an amazing journey for me. Along the way, I have received incredible support from too many people to acknowledge them all. I hope that everyone who has influenced and inspired me accepts my sincerest apologies if I have made mistakes, which are very much my own, and if I have not explicitly mentioned them. I am especially grateful to the officials and scholars in Europe and Southeast Asia who have been so kind to spare their valuable time to share their insights and allow me to indulge my inquisitive nature. I am truly indebted to the support that I have received from Jörn Dosch and Clara Portela. My gratitude also goes to the many institutions that have provided me with an academic home along the way. The National Centre for Research on Europe has been very kind to provide me with an institutional base to embark on my journey. In no particular order, the Centre for Southeast Asian Studies at the Albert-Ludwigs University in Freiburg, the Human Protection Hub and Griffith Asia Institúte at Griffith University in Brisbane, the EU Centre in Singapore, the International Institute for Strategic Studies, the EU Centre at Monash University in Melbourne and the European Commission-funded SEATIDE Network linked to the Centre for History and Economics at Cambridge University have been invaluable institutions for the realisation of my book project. Last, but not least, I would like to extend my sincerest thank you to my German family, my Thai family and my Kiwi family for their unconditional love and support.

Abbreviations

AECF	Asia Europe Cooperation Framework
AEMM	ASEAN–EU Ministerial Meeting
AFC	Asian Financial Crisis
AIPA	ASEAN Inter-parliamentary Assembly
AIPO	ASEAN Inter-parliamentary Organisation
AMM	Aceh Monitoring Mission
APEC	Asia-Pacific Economic Cooperation
APRIS	ASEAN–EU Programme for Regional Integration Support
ARF	ASEAN Regional Forum
ASEAN	Association of Southeast Asian Nations
ASEAN-PMC	ASEAN Post-Ministerial Conference
ASEAN ISIS	ASEAN Institutes of Strategic and International Studies
ASEM	Asia–Europe Meeting
ASEF	Asia–Europe Foundation
ATF	ASEM Asian Financial Crisis Trust Fund
CBM	confidence-building measure
CFSP	Common Foreign and Security Policy
CMI	Crisis Management Initiative
CSCE	Conference for Security and Cooperation in Europe
CSDP	Common Security and Defence Policy
CSO	civil society organisation
DFID	Department for International Development
DG	Directorate General
DG RELEX	Directorate General for External Relations
DIPECHO	Disaster Preparedness ECHO
DOM	Daerah Operasi Militer
EC	European Community
ECFIN	Economic and Financial Affairs

ECHO	European Commission's Humanitarian Office
EEAS	European External Action Service
EEC	European Economic Community
EFEX	European Financial Expertise Network
ESDP	European Security and Defence Policy
ESS	European Security Strategy
EU	European Union
FDI	foreign direct investment
FinMM	Finance Ministers' Meeting
FLEGT	Forest Law Enforcement, Governance and Trade
FMM	Foreign Ministers' Meeting
FTA	Free Trade Agreement
G7	Group of 7
G20	Group of 20
GAM	Free Aceh Movement
GFC	Global Financial Crisis
GIZ	Gesellschaft für Internationale Zusammenarbeit
GoI	Government of Indonesia
ICRC	International Committee of the Red Cross
IfS	Instrument for Stability
ILEA	International Law Enforcement Academy
IMF	International Monetary Fund
IMP	Initial Monitoring Presence
IPAP	International Promotion Action Plan
JCC	Joint Cooperation Committee
JCLEC	Jakarta Centre for Law Enforcement Cooperation
JI	Jemaah Islamiah
LoGA	Law on the Governance of Aceh
MDF	Multi Donor Fund
MDGs	Millennium Development Goals
MoU	Memorandum of Understanding
NATO	North Atlantic Treaty Organisation
NGO	non-governmental organisation
NTS	non-traditional security
OECD	Organisation for Economic Cooperation and Development
OPLAN	Operational Plan
ORHAP	Operational Regional Haze Action Plan
OSCE	Organisation for Security and Cooperation in Europe
PCA	Partnership and Cooperation Agreement
READI	Regional EU–ASEAN Dialogue Instrument
RHAP	Regional Haze Action Plan
RRM	Rapid Reaction Mechanism

SEARCCT	Southeast Asia Regional Centre for Counter Terrorism
SOM	Senior Officials' Meeting
TAM	Technical Assessment Mission
TFAP	Trade Facilitation Action Plan
TREATI	EU–ASEAN Trade Initiative
UN	United Nations
UNICEF	UN Children's Fund
UNSCR	UN Security Council Resolution
USA	United States of America
VDR	Voluntary Demonstration of Response
WTO	World Trade Organisation
YES	Yen-Euro-Dollar

Introduction

> One of the paradigm-shifts in how disasters are perceived and acted on was the Indian Ocean Tsunami in 2005. It became everyone's concern, no matter how far away you were.
>
> (Wahlström 2012)

The Boxing Day Tsunami of 2004 was shocking. News channels around the globe showed a wall of water swallowing coastlines across South and Southeast Asia, shattering the calm of the festive season in many parts of the world. Images of destruction triggered an outpouring of international solidarity on an unforeseen scale. The European Union (EU) was among the quickest in the international community to help the affected countries. National and regional initiatives to support the victims were launched and Europe appeared unified in its eagerness to help another region. On the regional level, Europe assisted promptly through the framework of the European Commission's Humanitarian Aid Office (ECHO), distributing funds to the United Nations (UN) and non-governmental organisations (NGOs) within 24 hours.

The European Commission itself granted €3 million to the International Committee of the Red Cross and activated the Community Civil Protection Mechanism which coordinated experts from various EU member states. By April 2005, the EU had activated three Rapid Reaction Mechanisms (RRMs) for the post-tsunami recovery and, by 15 December 2005, the European Commission had allocated over €100 million for humanitarian assistance to Asia. The European Commission further earmarked millions of euros for the post-tsunami rehabilitation and reconstruction.

In Southeast Asia, the Indonesian provinces of Aceh and Nias were particularly devastated and received considerable EU funding, mainly through the Multi Donor Fund (MDF). The European Commission co-chaired this Fund. MDF aimed to support a sustainable recovery and administered various projects, including the Reconstruction of Aceh

2 Introduction

Land Administration System Project; the Aceh Forest and Environment Programme; the Flood Mitigation Programme for Banda Aceh; the Tsunami Recovery Waste Management Programme, as well as the programme on Strengthening Civil Society Organisations in Community Recovery in Aceh and Nias. Overall, the contribution of the EU and its member states was said to have constituted 85 per cent of the total budget of the Fund (Delegation of the European Commission to Indonesia and Brunei Darussalam 2009). The EU's engagement in the aftermath of the Tsunami showed Southeast Asian countries that the EU is more than just an economic player: it is willing to provide aid when help is required (Maier-Knapp 2010).

At the same time, this catastrophe demonstrated the importance of regional arrangements and individual institutions located on the regional level. The European Commission was a significant orchestrator of assistance and complemented national efforts of the EU member states. Europe's engagement stimulated cooperative momentum, which went beyond disaster relief efforts and deepened the broader relationship between the regions.

A few months after the Tsunami struck, the EU became engaged in building and keeping peace in Aceh through the Aceh Monitoring Mission (AMM). The Nuremberg Declaration in 2007 and the subsequent Nuremberg Plan of Action built on this momentum and expanded the scope of interaction. The EU and Southeast Asia were increasingly working together to tackle the new challenges of the twenty-first century. Although the AMM provided impetus that enhanced the agenda and depth of the dialogue between the EU and the Association of Southeast Asian Nations (ASEAN), it did not attract sustained Southeast Asian interest in concrete follow-ups on peace-keeping. Overall, Europe continued to be perceived mainly through an economic lens. At the same time, the EU itself only sought to share its peace-keeping experiences with Southeast Asia on a sporadic basis. It was preoccupied with peace-keeping concerns closer to home.

This introductory discussion of the EU's engagement in the aftermath of the Boxing Day Tsunami raises some interesting questions:

> *Can the EU, a remote power, improve its profile as a collective (politico-security) actor through humanitarian and peace-keeping support in a region pre-occupied with strategic concerns?*
> *Can transboundary crises facilitate greater recognition of the EU as a political actor who seeks to project norms as well as act on the basis of its norms?*

What is the value of the existing ASEAN–EU dialogue as an institution for inter-regional cooperation? If crises function as stimulus for enhanced interaction within the ASEAN–EU relationship, does this indicate that the existing dialogue does not carry sufficient weight to further inter-regional communication and coordination?

To answer these questions, this book provides the first crisis-centric monograph about the EU as an actor in Southeast Asia and the EU's inter-regional activities. The book understands inter-regionalism to be the interaction between regional cooperative arrangements (Hänggi 2006; Söderbaum and van Langenhove 2006). Heiner Hänggi distinguishes between group-to-group, bi- and trans-regional and hybrid arrangements.[1] Jürgen Rüland has identified similar actor-centric typological arrangements for inter-regionalism, but has extended this categorisation with the concept of trans-regionalism. This concept describes a heterogeneous and diffuse arrangement between two regions with stakeholders from various levels of society and member states with overlapping regional memberships (Rüland 2002b).

The trans-regional and inter-regional forms of foreign policy are inherent and natural to the EU, because they legitimise and cement the EU's role as an international actor. As Frank Söderbaum explains,

> Thus, the EU's preference for region-building and interregionalism has implications not only for the foreign policy of the EU, but also for the organisation of the world polity where regional actors such as the EU gain legitimacy.
>
> (Söderbaum et al. 2006: 123)

Söderbaum implies that the supra-Westphalian organisational nature of the EU is reflected in the international structures and processes of which the EU is a part. At the same time, the EU is also being shaped by its interactions with its environment. In some instances, it may even be accused of emulating the features of a state. On the one hand, the EU displays an adaptive capacity within the Westphalian system. On the other, it promotes region-building to strengthen non-traditional actors of the Westphalian system. Thus, inter-regionalism provides a means to achieve twofold legitimacy.

This book is also sensitive to recent developments in Southeast Asia and draws upon cases of so-called non-traditional security (NTS)[2] crises in the 1990s and 2000s. Considering that European engagement with Southeast Asia in the context of these NTS crises post-Cold-War is shaped increasingly by an ethical understanding of security, this book implies a liberal-democratic agenda behind European efforts, aimed at strengthening the rights of people and the responsibilities of states. The EU attempts to pre-empt NTS crises and increase the overall welfare of states and their people through dialogue and cooperation on common challenges of the twenty-first century. While this human-centred perspective assists in improving cooperation between the two regions as well as the welfare in the partner region, it is to some extent a tacit continuation of the traditional donor–recipient relationship between the EU and Southeast Asia in light of the emphasis on development.

Of crises and non-traditional security

The case of the Boxing Day Tsunami underlines the important role of crises as catalysts for generating and enhancing intra-regional and inter-regional cooperative dynamics. In particular, it highlights how less institutionalised fora depend on the generation of cooperative momentum through crises. The following paragraphs outline the broader role crises play in relationship-building and the implications of NTS challenges for the EU as an actor in Southeast Asia.

In 1970, in the tradition of Ernst Haas – the father of neo-functionalist European integration theory – Philippe Schmitter observed the contingency of regional integration and crises:

> The process whereby an emerging regional center gains or loses in the scope or level of its authority vis-à-vis pre-existent national centers is best conceived as involving a series of crisis-provoked decisional cycles.
>
> (Schmitter 1970: 844)

Schmitter complemented the existing neo-functionalist body of literature, which was mainly concerned with categories of issue-/sector-specific cooperation and spill-over by incorporating a better understanding of the integrative dynamic itself and by emphasising the role of crises and feedback effects within these integrative processes.[3]

Crises represent situations where states as well as their regional institution revise behaviour and innovate strategies, or otherwise face disintegration. In order to prevent disintegration of established regional institutions, it is likely that states may consider overriding domestic constraints and suspending or replacing existing norms. Crisis situations legitimise change and can contribute to the expansion or decline of cooperation. They allow "institutions with an established reputation for efficiency and equity

[to] be called upon suddenly to take over other, crisis-ridden domains" (Schmitter 1970: 846). In this context, national and regional authorities may become more executive. Sometimes, they consider involving outside partners to assist and share their experience.

A crisis is perceived differently among actors. There is variation in the extent to which actors are affected or construct affectedness. The construction of crises by actors underlines the ability of crises to function like a magnifying glass: They bring out the vulnerabilities and shortcomings that have led to the construction of the crisis itself and stimulate corrective actions. Recognising the significance of crises as a tool to better grasp the behaviour of international actors allows a nuanced perspective on the dynamics of the EU's perceptions and behaviour towards Southeast Asia.

This crisis-centric perspective acknowledges that while the long-standing official dialogue between the two regions is shaped by the institutionalised formal engagement, there are irregular dynamics triggered by domestic, regional and international crises that influence and further the relationship: amid the problematic situation of the eurozone, the EU is pushing for greater engagement in Southeast Asia and has stepped up its diplomatic efforts through various high-level meetings with Southeast Asian leaders since 2012. It is increasingly giving attention to transboundary and unconventional security challenges including disaster relief, maritime security and the non-proliferation of weapons of mass destruction (WMD).

A decade ago, the Asian Financial Crisis (AFC) and the political stalemate on Myanmar ushered in a cooperative dynamic that displayed greater pragmatic and less politicised ties between the two regions. The AFC was a watershed event that challenged Southeast Asia's central normative tenets of non-interference and national sovereignty, which had underpinned Southeast Asia's minimalist approach to regional cooperation. The AFC compelled Southeast Asian political leaders to reconsider their approach. Greater interest in the European regional integrative experience arose among Southeast Asian officials. In turn, in the aftermath of the AFC, European politicians revised their view of Southeast Asia and sought to share their experience.

The EU believed that its prescription of regional integration could contribute to greater resilience of the ASEAN markets. This would also give some sense of market stability to the European side. According to the European Commission,

> the regional architecture in the region became more dynamic and people realised that ASEAN will remain in the centre.... I think it is

> fair to say that policy-makers in Europe became more alert about the region.... The economics are driving the relationship, it was recognised as a dynamic area, where the European Union should be involved, have more presence and the European Union should be more pragmatic...the [Asian Financial] Crisis played a role in the sense that it focused the people's minds on regional integration.
>
> (interview with European Commission official, 16 February 2009)

Parallel to the unfolding AFC in 1997, the ASEAN–EU relationship experienced a political crisis. The accession of Myanmar to ASEAN led to the postponement of the ASEAN–EU dialogue from 1997 to 1999. The terrorist attacks of September 11 in 2001 compelled the US to reposition Southeast Asia as the 'Second Front' in its 'War on Terror'. This had the effect of reinvigorating the security perspective towards Southeast Asia of some European states closely aligned with America.

The fourth critical politico-security cesura for the contemporary ASEAN–EU relationship was the case of the Boxing Day Tsunami, described previously as having enhanced cooperative efforts between the two regions. The end of the Cold War, the political stalemate on Myanmar, the September 11 attacks and the Boxing Day Tsunami were all major crises that impacted regional and inter-regional dynamics within the EU and ASEAN. These crises seem to have been decisive triggers for action, inaction and change of action, emphasising the need for a crisis-centric reconsideration of the EU as an actor in the region.

However, crises do not always enhance the cooperative dynamics and stimulate a 'paradigm shift'.[4] In fact, political crises on various levels have the potential to halt and even reverse cooperative advancements between the two regions – take, for instance, the aforementioned case of the ASEAN–EU dispute on Myanmar in 1997. Political crises on the domestic level, within individual ASEAN member states also had a share in impeding inter-regional integrative efforts. In 2009, Thailand was experiencing domestic political turmoil. It found it difficult to arrange the ASEAN Summit and the affiliated meetings with external partners. The domestic political issue complicated the ASEAN dialogue with third parties. These and many other domestic incidents display the importance of national and regional dynamics in Southeast Asia in shaping the EU's approach to the region. At the same time, EU domestic concerns also interfere with the relationship. The problems of the eurozone are intertwining acutely the economic and politico-security spheres, compelling the EU to gravitate towards Asia.

During the AFC, Europe had already realised that its own economic interests cannot be separated from Southeast Asia. The EU recognises that upholding its economic interests and sharing its experience of regional integration correlates with its own security concerns. Furthermore, it understands the covalence of ASEAN resilience and the stability of the wider East Asian region. This perspective implicitly recognises Southeast Asia as a security concern in a broad sense. That is, in an interdependent world, policy-makers and officials, in particular, argue that the security dimension cannot be separated from other spheres.

Security is an integral area of cooperation where the EU and Asia "have much experience to share and collaborative mechanisms to establish" (Segal and Shin 1997: 151). Issue-specific "security cooperation between Europe and East Asia has emerged as a central agenda in inter-regionalism and is likely to gain further importance" (Dosch 2003: 486). The dialogue and joint management of the newly emerging, transboundary and unconventional security concerns could advance the ASEAN–EU relationship and the EU as a politico-security actor (Yeo 2009; Maier-Knapp 2010).

The EU High Representative Catherine Ashton is one prominent European official figure promoting this perspective. At her first attendance at the Shangri-La Dialogue in 2013, she attempted to charm Asia-Pacific defence officials and outlined the EU's collective security perspective:

> We all face the same threats. Today I am here to reinforce our deep commitment to promoting global security and prosperity, not as an Asian power, but an Asian partner. We already have a partnership but I believe that we can do much more to deepen our cooperation even further....
>
> We believe we have a dual contribution to make to security in the region and beyond: first by offering to be a true long-term partner on security issues and second by being an effective and innovative one, through our ability to implement a comprehensive approach which is particularly suited to the new challenges we all face.
>
> Other speakers have already indicated and everyone in this room is aware that this century poses new security challenges that affect us all, everywhere in the world. We can only deal with them if we work together. So for us working with many Asian countries is an opportunity for cooperation and strong partnership to tackle common problems.
>
> Both the EU and Asia share the objective of securing peace and prosperity in our regions and beyond. We are partners facing global problems such as non-proliferation; terrorism and violent extremism; and we also jointly face the threats of climate change and energy security.
>
> (International Institute for Strategic Studies/Baroness Ashton 2013)

This is suggestive of an alternative and non-hegemonic security approach based on threat commonalities, primarily with a view towards issue-specific cooperation and dialogue. This EU approach is reminiscent of the confidence-building and pragmatic rationale behind the Conference for Security Cooperation in Europe/Organisation for Security Cooperation in Europe (CSCE/OSCE). It appears inherent in international actors who, firstly, have limited strategic outreach and, secondly, do not aspire to hegemony directly. European officials realise that they are not the "main flavour on the map" in Asia and that a stronger politico-security profile is intrinsically linked to the degree Europe can make its mark in the region in strategic and military terms (interview with EU official, 19 November 2009).

This book proposes that cooperation on NTS issues is crucial to the security of Southeast Asia. It aims to prove that this perspective incrementally strengthens the EU as a politico-security actor in the region. However, it also understands that an approach to Southeast Asia solely based on these concerns would fail to acknowledge the extent to which the security dynamics of the Asia-Pacific depend on power politics and military strength. Enhancing the EU's security footprint beyond this security 'light' approach is further complicated by the various stakeholders and alliances in the Asia-Pacific. For the time being, it appears that the EU aspires to complement the military might of the American hegemon. Another significant obstacle is the domestic circumstances of young sovereign states, unfavourable for external influence. While the AFC and other NTS issues may have sparked greater intra-regional transparency and coordination, overall, when looking at ASEAN's 'new' challenges, ranging from pollution to drug-trafficking to piracy, "one cannot escape noting that the room for influence from outside is generally rather limited" (Mahncke 1997: 8).

This book acknowledges these concerns and the sensitivity of non-interference. However, it must also be said that Southeast Asia is displaying greater awareness of insecurities that may lead to human suffering. There is growing institutional manifestation of this agenda on both the national and regional levels. The NTS perspective argues that this change originates in the inability of individual states to manage the challenges of the twenty-first century by themselves, leading to an adaptation in culture and behaviour, which then facilitates intra-regional cooperation and processes of convergence between Europe and Southeast Asia (Dosch 2003; Rüland 2005). At the same time, as Jörn Dosch cautions, converging security cultures will not necessarily translate into greater and deeper inter-regional security cooperation in the near future (Dosch 2003: 486).

From a human-oriented security perspective, European actors have contributed significantly to the stability of Southeast Asia, particularly through development cooperation. Generally speaking, the EU sees its human-oriented security engagement in the context of development and humanitarian assistance. Indeed, the framing of the case studies in this book as so-called NTS issues instead of human security threats is in keeping with the Southeast Asian state-centred perspective.

However, this NTS perspective poses a conceptual conundrum for the EU, since it premises that humanitarianism and security coincide *per se*. In fact, introducing the concept of non-traditional development (NTD) may capture the essence of the EU's contributions more appropriately. This discussion further raises the question whether the EU has actually used this highly political NTS frame at all to actively assist Southeast Asia and strengthen the politico-security profile of the EU and its member states. Adopting the NTS lens implies that Europe accepts the Southeast Asian perspective. While NTS has been increasingly incorporated into the official dialogue this is not to say that the EU condones a securitised perspective on what it perceives as developmental or humanitarian concerns.

In light of this conceptual ambiguity and the crisis-centric dynamic of the ASEAN–EU relationship, analysing the extent to which the EU has made an impact in Southeast Asia from an NTS perspective systematically is timely and urgently needed. Understanding the way NTS challenges have been perceived and dealt with in the past gives us insights into contemporary inter-regional behaviour and attitudes. To understand the present, we need to look backwards and learn. The future direction of the EU as an actor in Southeast Asia is interwoven with these historical moments in time, where disputes and ideational tensions between the two regions have been overcome and cooperative efforts launched.

The book begins with a discussion of the analytical context providing an overview of the ASEAN–EU relationship. The historical overview touches on the trade and aid dimensions, but in contrast to the existing scholarship, it assumes a politico-security perspective. This is followed by a discussion of the official EU security perspective towards Southeast Asia and the major instruments that the EU has at its disposal as a so-called collective 'NTS actor' or 'actor on NTS threats'. This last distinction is worth paying attention to since the conception of the EU as an NTS actor has to be consistent with the overall goals of the EU as an actor. This framework implies that the EU conducts its actions through an NTS lens. Conversely, the framing of the EU as an actor concerned with NTS challenges suggests that the EU acts to address a specific issue identified generally, or by its counterpart, as belonging to NTS.

Having established the context, the succeeding chapters tell the story of selected NTS crises throughout the 1990s and 2000s, focusing on the EU's engagement. I treat these crises in chronological order, beginning with the AFC in 1997 and the haze in 1997, then moving on to the Bali Bombings in October 2002, the avian influenza outbreak of 2003 and the political conflict in Aceh. The narrative involves crises that are generally 'low politics', transboundary, of sudden onset and posing a threat to both the state and society. They cover a broad spectrum of NTS crises post-Cold War to allow a systematic assessment of *Southeast Asia and the European Union: non-traditional security crises and cooperation*. These cases provide specific insights into: (a) the extent of EU responsive action based on threat perceptions and interdependence; (b) the operational and toolkit preference of the EU; and (c) the constraints to its activities.

Chapters 2 and 3 discuss NTS crises that occurred in the tragic year of 1997. This year marked ASEAN's official orientation towards greater intra-regional coordination and integration. These two chapters, firstly, outline the NTS challenge and ASEAN's regional integrative dynamics in the aftermath of the individual crises. Then, they discuss the EU's engagement and, furthermore, assess the extent to which the ideational dimension of the EU as an actor influenced its cooperative behaviour with Southeast Asia.

Chapter 4 draws upon the case of the Bali Bombings in 2002 and the avian influenza outbreak of 2003. These challenges occurred in the aftermath of the September 11 attacks, in a time of heightened insecurity perceptions among Western countries. Against this backdrop of pervasive insecurity, the chapter seeks to shed light on the EU's engagement. This allows us to grasp the extent to which the European perspective entails growing politicisation and securitisation towards Southeast Asia. The chapter discusses the Bali Bombings and examines the EU's inter-regional and selected bilateral activities to assist the ASEAN region. This is followed by an investigation into European assistance and its role in combating the avian influenza outbreak in Southeast Asia. Central to these cases is the role of threat perceptions in discerning the cooperative dynamics.

Chapter 5 delves into the one and only Common Security and Defence Policy (CSDP) mission to Southeast Asia. It highlights the gap between the EU's value-guided identity and the extent to which the EU's norms and values can be implemented in CSDP operations. The succeeding chapter outlines more contemporary NTS challenges pertaining to the ASEAN–EU agenda. These include disaster relief, food security and maritime security. The chapter, then, restates the main determinants of EU action in light of the NTS crises in Southeast Asia. Finally, this book concludes with an overview of its central findings, the implications of the NTS perspective for the newly created European External Action Service (EEAS) and for the debate on the EU as a politico-security actor in world affairs.

Notes

1 The first arrangement is associated with old regionalism and the European Economic Community. It describes the inter-regional relations between two regional organisations such as the ASEAN–EU dialogue in this thesis. The second arrangement is related to the post-Cold War triadisation of world economy. The actors involved can belong to more than two regions and do not necessarily have to represent a pre-existing regional organisation. The third constellation characterises the relations between a regional organisation/group and a single power.
2 NTS is understood to be a security concept relating to the extensive array of post-Cold War threats that are neither state-to-state nor military in nature. NTS challenges refer to security risks and threats that have been caused by a non-military security source, which are not contained by national borders. Among Southeast Asian scholars and officials, this security concept has been commonly used to describe the new types of security threats, since the Asian Financial Crisis occurred and contested traditional modes of cooperation and security understanding. The concept implies that security to address these threats goes beyond traditional security and holds the potential to accommodate both state and non-state actors as the security providers.
3 In simple terms, these core categories of neo-functionalism describe the extent to which integration is facilitated and contingent on specific areas of common concern within the low politics. According to neo-functionalists such as Ernst Haas or Leon Lindberg, this cooperation leads to cooperative and integrative dynamics on issues in other areas that are linked to this initial area of integration.
4 In the introductory citation by UN Special Representative on Disaster Relief Reduction Wahlström, natural disasters were described as crises with the potential to lead to paradigmatic shifts.

1 Introduction to the analytical and historical context

Europeans have romanticised Asia since the days of the Silk Road and the adventures of Marco Polo. Against the backdrop of the eurozone crisis, this perspective has given way to a more sober view. Today, European states and institutions are discovering Southeast Asia through a comprehensive partnership, ranging from trade relations to security affairs. In this book, the NTS frame underpins the ASEAN–EU partnership. It suggests that cooperation with Southeast Asian states serves to raise the levels of welfare among the partners. At the same time, it implies that the partner is a security 'threat' or under-developed and inferior.

By portraying and perceiving challenges in Southeast Asia as challenges for themselves, European officials and publics move beyond the recognition of interdependence. They redefine and rethink concepts of Europe and Southeast Asia politically. Frank Umbach explains,

> With the waves of the Asian crisis of 1997–98 and the terrorist attack on September 11, 2001, and its impact on Asia, European politicians and the public have begun to recognise that despite the geographical and psychological distance of many local and regional conflicts from Europe, they have and will have direct or at least indirect impacts on Europe's future economic and political stability.
>
> (Umbach 2004: 10)

While Umbach refers to the psychological distance inherent in the relationship, this book assumes that emotional and ideational distance can be overcome through interdependence. In this context, interdependence entails increased geographical porosity and the meeting of different ideas, values and norms. Yet, ideational and emotional attachments may also be sharpened and radicalised when confronted with other ideas, values and norms. This could shape defensive attitudes and regional bulwarks. It can trigger the formation of non-governmental interest groups countering the rise of inter-regional cooperation. Such groups could easily coalesce across national borders. In light of these scenarios, the consequences of interdependence are ambiguous for the EU in Southeast Asia.

The importance of interdependence for international actors suggests that insecurity stems to some extent from the way we socially interact, interpret and perceive the world. Hence, security and insecurity are highly constructed social notions, irrespective of the tangible military dimension of security. Despite adopting a security prism in the broadest sense, this study is critical of the extent to which interdependence encourages the transcendence of insecurity perceptions and the recalibration of new forms of structural dominance within asymmetrical partnerships. That is, this book aims to raise awareness about the way regional and inter-regional integrative dynamics are justified by a heightened sense of insecurity, which simultaneously appears normalised and increasingly integrated and articulated as day-to-day politics.

Securitisation is an important concept in this context. It is a prominent technology that refers to the process of threat construction and the way speech acts can affect a rising level of urgency around a particular issue (Buzan et al. 1998: 23–26). It describes the way political figures construct threats with the affirmation and approval of an audience. Securitisation either promotes an existing security concern to a higher level of priority or recasts a traditionally non-security issue as an existential threat requiring an emergency response. Securitisation, then, can be defined,

> as a more extreme version of politicization ... [that] is constituted by the intersubjective establishment of an existential threat with a saliency sufficient to have substantial political effects.... A successful securitization thus has three components (or steps): existential threats, emergency action, and effects on interunit relations by breaking free of rules.
>
> (Buzan et al. 1998: 23–26)

Securitisation is a speech act that can be used at any level of society, although its most successful employers are political leaders pressing for some issues to become an urgent security concern. Securitisation is also highly dependent on epistemic communities which can identify and pre-define threats. A good example of this is the relationship between researchers and their benefactors, which may pre-determine the selection of particular threats and preclude others from examination and debate.

Securitisation is a common tool – although a problematic tool used by international actors to push their agenda, not least in Southeast Asia (Emmers 2004; Tow 2004). It legitimises increased security activities that are ultimately aimed at protecting certain political communities.

It is exactly this legitimisation and eventual normalisation of, as a rule, coercive and illiberal instruments that concerns some EU scholars and officials involved in development and humanitarian cooperation with Southeast Asia.

Securitisation generally implies a military and technocratic management approach based on expert knowledge. This is to some extent at odds with the democratic values at the heart of the European project. NTS may obfuscate the EU's normative agenda in its relations with Southeast Asia. Likewise, NTS has ramifications for the security-development nexus. Emphasising the intersection of the development and security spheres risks the further politicisation of the issue area and leads to normative conflict within the EU's internal and external identity.

The securitisation of cooperation between the EU and Southeast Asia jeopardises the carefully crafted image of the EU as a norm- and value-guided actor. This compels us to investigate the normative tensions that arise from the adoption of the NTS perspective, which implies mainly tacit politicisation and securitisation processes. Specifically, this book contributes to the scholarly debate concerned with the role of the EU as a promoter of norms in Southeast Asia. This literature agrees that the EU *does* strategise about the deployment of its norms and values – more or less successfully – to assume a greater role in the region.

Given the implications of securitisation and politicisation associated with the NTS concept, this book necessitates a theoretical approach that captures processes of normative influence and change. For this reason, I employ a two-pronged reflectivist approach based on constructivism and social action theory to examine the EU as an actor and its impact in Southeast Asia.

This study is part of the growing body of international relations literature that draws upon constructivist theorising to capture the importance of ideas as shapers of the behaviour of actors. It recognises that whatever actors do, their actions are always interdependent and embedded in some kind of normative context. The rise of constructivism in the scholarship of the ASEAN–EU relationship is associated with various events in the 1990s that culminated in the Asian value debate and the clash over Myanmar's accession to ASEAN.

Constructivism in combination with social action theory enables us to gauge the relationship between normative identity, interaction and outcome of action. Constructivism acknowledges that the ideational context steers actors towards certain behaviour. Understanding the cultural context of threat perceptions allows for a more nuanced account of the EU's actions. Social action theory focuses on the relationship between normative input and normative output. While constructivism addresses the

The analytical and historical context 15

capacity of the EU to project norms in its external relations, social action theory pre-defines the normative as well as rationalist mode of action from an EU-as-agent perspective. Social action theory assists in distinguishing between the rationales, types, motivations and the impact of actions. This book applies social action theory in the sense that it allows the identification of cost-benefit rationales underlying the normative dimension of the EU's actions.

To accommodate to this actor-centric approach, this book views the EU as an actor with and within Southeast Asia, primarily through the European Commission and places particular emphasis on the threat perceptions, actions, inactions and interactions of the European Commission in relation to the selected NTS crises. On the secondary level, it takes into account the activities of the member states. This perspective recognises that the EU has become an actor in its own right in world affairs. However, it is not always clear whether the EU is an actor or merely a presence in Southeast Asia (Maier-Knapp 2012). This is particularly the case when the term 'presence' is seemingly interchangeable with the term 'actor' in scholarly debates (Allen and Smith 1991; Allen and Smith 1998).

Indeed, the concept of presence has been extended to "making one's presence felt", which includes more tangible aspects of presence (Allen and Smith 1998: 53). Expanding the concept in this way coheres with this book's understanding of an actor; that is, being identifiable, being able to aggregate interests and having the ability to formulate and implement goals (Rüland 2002a: 10; Bretherton and Vogler 2006). This book understands an actor narrowly in relation to specific NTS contexts, based on the selected NTS case studies only. These case studies are discussed in the chapters that follow. But first, before delving into these case studies, it is important to outline the general historical and politico-security context of the EU's relationship with Southeast Asia.

The historical context of the ASEAN–EU relationship

Informal meetings between the European Economic Community (EEC) and the ministerial delegation of ASEAN in Brussels on 16 June 1972, in Bangkok on 5 and 6 September 1973 and in Jakarta on 24 and 25 September 1974 paved the way for the formal biannual ministerial meetings[1] between the two regional groupings, beginning in 1978. At the second ministerial meeting in Kuala Lumpur, the relationship was divided into two official tracks: the inter-regional dialogue and the Joint Cooperation Committee (JCC).[2] The European Community's (EC) institutionalised approach to Southeast Asia had been part of a wider strategy to manage development and trade relations with developing countries in the Cold War period. In this context, it also needs to be highlighted that the EC saw Southeast Asia as part of a greater Asian strategy to contain the Communist threat emanating from China (interview with former Commission official working for Wilhelm Haferkamp, 15 February 2009). Southeast Asian governments welcomed this engagement, which strengthened their own strategy to contain China.

In spite of the looming Communist threat, the early ministerial meetings displayed a strong focus on economic issues (ASEAN and EC ministers 1974: para. 5). ASEAN member states were eager to gain market access to the newly created European market bloc. In the early years, the Commission of the European Communities was interested in strengthening its external role and trade competence. The EEC member states showed less interest in Asia and paid greater attention to the former colonies in Africa and the oil-exporting countries (interview with former Commission official working for Wilhelm Haferkamp, 15 February 2009).

At the same time, the market-based approach of the Southeast Asian states was driven by a sense of envy and neglect, dubbed "*Afrikaneid*"[3] by some former European Commission officials (interview with former Commission official working for Wilhelm Haferkamp, 15 February 2009). Believing that they were entitled to the same benefits as other developing countries, Southeast Asian governments hoped that the market-based approach to the EC would yield better preferential treatment and economic gains. Economic interests dominated the agenda and led to a special ASEAN–EC Ministerial Meeting on Economic Matters in 1985. During this time, there was only one politico-security concern placed on the ASEAN–EC agenda: the conflict in Indochina and the resulting refugee problem (ASEAN and EC member states 1978).

The ASEAN–EC meetings established confidence and allowed an exchange of ideas. This dialogue format consists of the foreign ministers of the regions. As a natural result of the political competence of the representatives and the growing trust among them, the political agenda broadened incrementally in the mid-1980s and a wider range of international political issues was incorporated into the agenda. While Southeast Asia's dialogue with the Commission of the European Communities remained focused on trade, the ASEAN–EC Ministerial Meetings expanded the discussion of international politico-security issues.

The Joint Statement on Political Issues in 1980 was the starting point for this development. This statement reiterated the principles of cooperation, which included human rights, standards of national sovereignty and the prime role of the UN. It contained a common position on the invasions in Kampuchea and Afghanistan. The Kampuchean problem posed an immediate threat to ASEAN's stability and tested the national, regional and international capacity – including that of the EC member states. The EC member states supported the ASEAN position in the UN and contributed financially to the UN missions to solve the refugee and displaced persons problem in Kampuchea and neighbouring countries. Both sides were deeply concerned about this situation and the concomitant expansion of the Communist threat. The Paris Agreements temporarily ended the instability of Indochina and eased concerns on both sides.

The Kampuchean issue heightened the importance of Southeast Asian security to Europe (Palmujoki 2001: 98). The ideological reality of the Cold War facilitated the conceptualisation of a common strategic interest. Both the EC and ASEAN member states pursued an anti-Soviet policy. The Soviet naval expansion in the Pacific, the Vietnamese invasion of Kampuchea and the Soviet invasion of Afghanistan were key concerns to both sides. In view of the common threat perceptions and the systemic reality, there was the real possibility of a nascent ASEAN–European security community (Peou 2002).

The American withdrawal from Indochina and the increasing economic interdependence between the two regions were further developments that triggered greater inclusion of the politico-security dimension. Eventually, bipolarity came to an end and the common antagonist disappeared. Post-Cold War NTS issues were increasingly incorporated into the agenda of the ASEAN–EC dialogue and posed a new opportunity for a common strategic interest. At the same time, the ideological differences between the two regions, previously muted by the Communist threat, became more apparent.

The diverging stance on China in the aftermath of the Tiananmen Massacre of 1989 was an appetiser for the contention on human rights between the two regions in the years to come. Since then, the ASEAN–EC/EU relations have been gradually, but constantly, strained by the EC's/EU's normative agenda. Gabriela Manea observed that "ASEAN's confrontational mode of interaction with the European Union regarding human rights policy has been a catalyst for the dynamic growth of a collective definition of self for ASEAN" (Manea 2008: 370). She further stated that this process has "contributed to the development of a communicative space for negotiating human rights issues at a regional level, which has been central to the gradual transformation of ASEAN's collective identity formation" (Manea 2008: 370). The ASEAN–EU relationship and other relations with Western powers have contributed to a greater intra-regional human rights discourse. At the same time, this ideational confrontation has crystallised a distinct 'Asian Way' prominently advocated by Malaysian Prime Minister Mohammad Mahathir.

At the 11th AEMM in Karlsruhe, as well as in the New Asia Strategy of 1994, the EU member states recognised the limits of their promotion of human rights and political conditionality. This politicised mode of interaction had not yielded significant economic benefits from the booming Southeast Asian economies and the EU retreated to a more pragmatic approach. In particular, the creation of the Asia-Pacific Economic Cooperation (APEC) group compelled the EU to rethink its approach and refocus on competitiveness. In spite of increasing pragmatism on the side of the EU, Myanmar's accession to ASEAN in 1997 faced strong European objections. By politicising Myanmar, the EU alienated the ASEAN member states. This political dispute came at a time when initial cracks were seen in Southeast Asia's economic miracle.

Europe's humanitarian concern about Myanmar was longstanding. Since the violent crackdown on pro-democracy protesters in 1988, European institutions and publics had been vocal in condemning the anti-democratic developments and human rights abuses in the country. A series of sanctions was launched in the 1990s. Myanmar's accession to ASEAN was discussed in the same year the EU upgraded fundamental rights to EU law with the Treaty of Amsterdam. As a result of the accession, there was the prospect that Myanmar would be defended by ASEAN officially. This immediately soured the relationship between the two regions to the extent that the official dialogue was suspended (Petersson 2006).

ASEAN remained determined to resolve the Myanmar issue on its own terms and did not succumb to external pressure. ASEAN members believed that by integrating Myanmar into their association, Myanmar would be forced to socialise and abandon its isolationist foreign policy. To this end, Thai Foreign Minister Surin Pitsuwan adapted Malaysia's Deputy Prime Minister Anwar Ibrahim's concept of constructive intervention, which was originally proposed to assist Cambodia's reforms. He advocated a policy based on 'flexible engagement' (Pitsuwan 12 June 1998). But this form of engagement circumvented the principle of non-interference by advocating 'peer pressure' and 'friendly advice', and hence received little support within ASEAN. Indonesian Foreign Minister Ali Alatas urged Pitsuwan to tone down the language and to use the notion of 'enhanced interaction' (Chalermpalanupap 2010: 154). This was in tune with ASEAN's main objective of socialising Myanmar and avoided an invasive strategy of pressuring Myanmar to act in a certain way.

An ASEAN member state official admitted that in spite of this strategy of socialisation, progress in Myanmar had not been apparent, and thus the EU had "rightly criticised" and "lectured" ASEAN (interview with ASEAN member state official, 21 November 2008).

However, Singapore, Malaysia and other countries have also assumed a critical stance towards Myanmar (Dosch 2008: 539). In particular, in informal bilateral dialogues with Myanmar, some ASEAN countries have been more candid in expressing their concerns to the officials of the military junta (interview with ASEAN member state official, 21 November 2008). Southeast Asian governments do not disagree with the EU on Myanmar, but prefer a less confrontational method. Between 1997 and 1999 this difference in approach put the ASEAN–EU relationship in jeopardy and some Southeast Asians felt that the EU was abusing its dominant power position within the ASEAN–EU relationship. An ASEAN member state official suggested that Myanmar became a burden to the relationship, because the ASEAN–EU dialogue consists of "a smaller group than [Asia–Europe Meeting] ASEM; and at ASEM there are more political and security issues of greater importance" (interview with ASEAN member state official, 21 November 2008). In spite of the EU's initial political rejection of Myanmar within ASEM, the EU acknowledged the open and informal format of ASEM and accepted Myanmar's participation.

The EU gradually accepted the ASEAN Way to manage Myanmar. A European official explained this pragmatic turn:

> Just a few years back, most political meetings were dominated by the discussion on Myanmar, now, at the Summit or Ministerial level, most of our Ministers or officials had to make statement about Myanmar in EU–ASEAN meetings and you know this created bad partnership, lack of faith, and, now, we again make the point on Myanmar, but meetings are not just dominated by it. We make our point, but we understand ASEAN's constraints as well.... It is an issue, but since it does not dominate meetings as it did a few years back, it makes our cooperation easier and, therefore more fruitful.
>
> (interview with European Commission official, 20 February 2009)

The EU is now pursuing a stance towards Myanmar that is more compatible with ASEAN's notion of enhanced interaction. Another European Commission official suggested that "we must learn to speak to Myanmar in order to achieve our objective: greater democratisation and so on. And the dialogue with ASEAN enabled us to appreciate how we can engage with Myanmar in a more positive sense" (interview with European Commission official, 20 February 2009). In fact, the recent positive developments in Myanmar could be suggestive of the success of ASEAN's approach of socialisation. The EU has suspended and lifted sanctions and, furthermore, toned down its rhetoric on Myanmar as a threat to ASEAN security. In the past, the official rhetoric of the EU has highlighted Myanmar as a fragile and vulnerable state representing a major source of NTS threats to Southeast Asia (European Commission 2003). At the same time, NTS issues have provided an avenue through which the EU has assisted the people of Myanmar. The EU has provided humanitarian assistance to Myanmar since 1994 through ECHO.

From the 1990s until the early 2010s, the production and smuggling of narcotics, HIV and AIDS, cross-border incursions, and refugee flows to neighbouring countries were recurring themes addressed within the ASEAN–EU dialogue, outlining the threat Myanmar posed to regional security. In fact, the issue of Myanmar was the only Southeast Asian security concern mentioned in the revised report of the European Security Strategy (European Council 2008: 11). This insecurity has not subsided, but the EU's attitude towards Myanmar has changed significantly.

The ASEAN members hold the responsibility to socialise and, when necessary, effectively punish their fellow members. Socialisation may have worked to some extent in the case of Myanmar, since seemingly "constructive engagement offered a means to persuade the military regime to allow international humanitarian aid into Myanmar" (Cook 2010: 435). Europeans admitted in the aftermath of Cyclone Nargis that humanitarian access was facilitated by ASEAN's socialisation approach (interview with EU official, 5 February 2009). Nevertheless, effective monitoring and penalising has been non-existent within ASEAN regional cooperation: ASEAN member states were and are reluctant to interfere in the domestic governance of partner ASEAN countries, while the ASEAN Charter as a regional sanctioning document lacks teeth and fails to function as a deterrent to non-complying ASEAN member states.

The EU continues to be concerned about human rights abuses by the military in Myanmar and counts continuously on the engagement of non-state actors or state-affiliated organisations to provide assistance to the people. This strategy circumvents lenience in the EU's and member states' official standing towards Myanmar. Values and principles are seemingly upheld. While this does not entirely resolve the normative dilemma that the EU faces, it alleviates the plight of the people of Myanmar.

The case of Myanmar clearly demonstrates that NTS is an important political frame and that ideational factors do indeed act as shapers of behaviour within the ASEAN–EU relationship. The ideological convergence during the Cold War and divergence in its aftermath suggest that ideational contexts and normative identities of international actors are powerful variables in understanding their behaviour.

The historical overview of the ASEAN–EU dialogue has displayed three different phases of the relationship from a politico-security perspective. During the Cold War, the superpower overlay determined the central security issues. These were mainly the flow of Indochinese refugees and the Communist expansions with the invasions in Kampuchea and Afghanistan (ASEAN and EC member states 1978: para. 13; ASEAN and EC member states 1980). By the 4th ASEAN–EC Ministerial Meeting on 25 March 1983 in Bangkok, the agenda broadened in geographical scope and addressed problematic developments in other regions of the world (ASEAN and EC member states 1983: para. 20). By the 6th ASEAN–EC Ministerial Meeting of 20–21 October 1986 in Jakarta, horizontal matters became more important. NTS threats, including narcotics and international terrorism, were now actively integrated into the agenda, although the NTS concept was not yet introduced.

This second phase of deeper and wider cooperation from the early to mid-1980s onwards benefitted from the confidence-building efforts between the two regions during the early years. Mutual trust was further boosted by the common Communist threat. At the same time, on the international level, the policy of détente enabled foreign ministers to move beyond the discussion of issues related to the Cold War structure. The method of issue-specific and pragmatic dialogue on common concerns postulated by the CSCE became the standard approach underpinning the EC's external relations and de-emphasised the enmity–amity structure of the Cold War.

At the 7th ASEAN–EC Ministerial Meeting, the politico-security agenda was extended to include disarmament and arms control. The ending of the Cold War was near and NTS issues ranging from international terrorism to environmental degradation became a greater concern to both sides. After the Cold War, the dialogue continued to deepen and broaden. This third phase was characterised by substantive and functional post-Cold War cooperation between the two sides. Various new mechanisms were introduced, including the Trans-Regional EU–ASEAN Trade Initiative (TREATI) and Regional EU–ASEAN Dialogue Instrument (READI).

In line with liberalism's triumph, NTS concerns became more important. Environmental protection was brought onto the agenda of the ASEAN–EU Ministerial Meeting in 1992, prior to the Rio Summit (ASEAN and EC member states 1991: para. 61–64). In 1994, the Karlsruhe Declaration further recognised the significance of the EU interacting with Southeast Asia. However, the impetus of the Karlsruhe Declaration was short-lived and a new dynamic was urgently needed. In the early 2000s, the ASEAN–EU Ministerial Meetings touched upon the NTS concept and proposed that, future co-operation should focus on non-traditional security issues, establishing channels of communication between the ASEAN Secretariat and relevant EU counterparts as well as environmental and cultural co-operation. This co-operation in areas of priority for both ASEAN and EU will be based on a practical and flexible approach, and will be jointly developed and implemented.

(ASEAN and EU member states, 27–28 January 2003: para. 9)

NTS was an opportunity to conduct pragmatic issue-oriented cooperation; however, European foreign ministries remained reserved about the utility of the concept.

With the Nuremberg Declaration and the subsequent Plan of Action to Implement the Nuremberg Declaration in 2007, both regions attempted to reignite the partnership in a manner that continued along the lines of issue-specific and pragmatic cooperation in support of the ASEAN community-building process (ASEAN–EU member states 2007: Joint Action 1.2). In terms of NTS issues, the Plan prioritised crisis management and conflict prevention as well as capacity building. It defined international terrorism, transnational crime and disarmament, arms control and the non-proliferation of weapons of mass destruction (WMD) as the central security concerns. The Plan further restated the ASEAN Regional Forum (ARF) as the primary security dialogue forum including NTS threats in Southeast Asia. Both ASEAN and EU member states expressed willingness to increase joint hostings of ARF seminars and workshops. This intention was translated into practice with the ARF Seminar to Enhance Maritime Security from 5 to 6 March 2009 in Surabaya (EU–Indonesia) and numerous other joint activities of the Indicative Lists of Activities 2007–2008, 2009–2010 and 2011–2012.

The Plan and the Indicative Lists of Activities bridge between the ASEAN and EU understandings of security and attempt to incorporate activities that involve multiple stakeholders and levels of governance. Activity V of the Indicative List of Activities 2009–2010 states that the two sides should continue promoting dialogue and partnership among private sectors, civil societies and other relevant organisations to facilitate new ideas and methods with a view towards enhancing transparency, accountability, participatory and effective governance. In theory, the NTS concept leaves room for actors other than the state and military to become engaged in managing the threats.

Many countries are facing a catalogue of similar threats transcending the requirement of conventional national defence. However, the reality in Southeast Asia is that the military is the only currently existing institution in the majority of countries that is trained, disciplined and equipped enough to respond effectively to the various NTS crises affecting Southeast Asia. The NTS crises in the region have revealed that in many ASEAN countries, the military is embedded in the government of the state. Even in so-called Southeast Asian democracies, the military solution is considered for an extensive spectrum of NTS threats. Despite some technical similarity in response between the EU and Southeast Asia and the convergence of threat perceptions of the two regions, Southeast Asian responses have remained concentrated on state-centric approaches (Rüland 2005).

Cooperation implies that shared experiences, information and best practices are embedded in specific cultural contexts. This suggests that the EU as an actor can exert normative influence even through technical and issue-specific cooperation. For this kind of influence to gain traction, the ASEAN side has to be receptive to the EU's principles and norms. The EU is an actor with deeply entrenched values and principles. These include multilateralism with UN primacy; peaceful settlements and solutions; reluctance about the use of force; the mainstreaming of human rights; cooperation with other actors; and pre-emption. There are some democratising ASEAN member states that promote a similar normative agenda and receive considerable European financial assistance.

In practice, the EU finds it difficult to reflect all values and principles consistently, as will be discussed in greater detail in the case of the AMM in Chapter 5. Securitisation, in particular, obfuscates the EU's normative and principled external identity. By lowering the threshold of what is considered as security, the EU risks undercutting its moral high ground. Since the EU is dependent on garnering influence through attraction and persuasion, securitisation has provoked accusations of double standards and hypocrisy in the EU's external relations. For instance, developing countries in Southeast Asia have been frequently confused by the EU's and some member states' inconsistency in promoting human rights.

In the document A New Partnership with South East Asia (COM (2003) 399/4), the EU officially recognised ASEAN as an important trading partner to the EU and a region that required security assistance (European Commission 2003). This document signalled the EU's willingness to assist the region on a variety of concerns, including NTS issues. It was indicated that the EU would pursue active talks and cooperation with ASEAN states on these challenges. The European Commission Communication COM (2003) 399/4 identified the phenomenon of terrorism as an important strategic aspect of Southeast Asia, although EU member states did not necessarily agree upon the extent to which Southeast Asian terrorist groups had international connections. It listed terrorism among the EU's top security priorities in the region. In the communication, the EU acknowledged the linkage between terrorism/

24 *The analytical and historical context*

extremism and development in a comprehensive manner, and a sum of €21 million was designated to support counter-terrorist projects in Southeast Asia (European Commission 2003: 13).

The communication explicitly said that one of the EU's main motivations for an enhanced partnership with Southeast Asia is the economic and trade interests with the region (European Commission 2003: 6). This interest was in sync with the economic interest on the ASEAN side. At the same time, the document stressed that shared values and common political and economic interests are the guarantors for enhanced cooperation between ASEAN and the EU (European Commission 2003: 11). Additionally, being a European Commission document, the communication underlined that the ASEAN–EU inter-regional dialogue should not thoroughly discuss security issues of a global or wider regional concern, since these issues are better addressed in the ARF and ASEM frameworks (European Commission 2003: 23). In an era of transboundary and common challenges, this rhetoric referring to other multilateral frameworks limits the development of the ASEAN–EU politico-security dialogue. It indicates the contingency of the politico-security agenda on the will and direction of the member states and their bilateral interests. It is also a document that reveals the fine balancing act of the European Commission in juggling the development and security agendas, albeit with emphasis on the former.

Since 2003, the EU's strategy towards Southeast Asia has undergone significant changes. The drafting of the ASEAN Charter and the ASEAN community-building process necessitated a new approach. This was pursued in the form of the Regional Strategy Paper 2007–2013 for Southeast Asia and the Plan of Action of Nuremberg. In October 2009, the first ever visit of the chairman of the EU Military Committee to the ASEAN Secretariat signalled to ASEAN that CSDP is interested in defence and security cooperation on NTS issues and willing to take the ASEAN–EU relationship further. The NTS issues talked about were maritime security, disaster relief and peace support operations. In 2011, EU Commissioner for International Cooperation, Humanitarian Aid and Crisis Response, Kristalina Georgieva, was the first EU Commissioner to visit the ASEAN Secretariat and discuss greater cooperative efforts in regional best practice-sharing and joint training exercises in civil protection.

Theoretically, the EU possesses the instruments and resources to assist with these kinds of NTS challenges and be an important partner to Southeast Asia. This view was further underlined by High Representative Catherine Ashton of the EU at the 12th Shangri-La Dialogue in 2013.

> Our strength lies in our ability to respond to a crisis with a wide range of tools and instruments, short and long term, humanitarian and

development, security and political. We call this the comprehensive approach, an approach that we believe is particularly suited to tackling the new security challenges we face today. For us the comprehensive approach implies combining hard and soft power to achieve lasting security and prosperity. This approach, we believe, makes us a unique global partner for Asia on security issues.

(International Institute for Strategic Studies/Baroness Ashton 2013)

Instruments pertinent to non-traditional security challenges

The preference for certain resources and operational modes points to the ideational dimension underlying EU action. The following paragraphs will discuss the major collective instruments that the EU has at its disposal to address NTS issues. Firstly, there is the aforementioned CSDP, which is the primary intergovernmental and collective body with civilian and military capabilities. In 2005, CSDP was deployed to Southeast Asia for the first time. In this case, it was the civilian arm of CSDP that acted. The CSDP is a post-Cold War military construct tailored for an environment in which the "neat dividing lines between hard and soft security, civil and military are rapidly dissolving, requiring far more flexibility on the part of Western state security institutions than has hitherto been the case" (Lindley-French 2005: 2).

Amid the war in the Balkans, the EU member states recognised that the ultimate concern for them must be a common autonomous military power "in order to promote peace, security and progress in Europe and in the world" (European Council 1992). At the Cologne Summit in 2003, it was declared,

> the European Union shall play its full role on the international stage. To that end, we intend to give the European Union the necessary means and capabilities to assume its responsibilities regarding a common European policy on security and defence.... The Union must have the capacity for autonomous action, backed up by credible military forces, the means to decide to use them, and a readiness to do so, in order to respond to international crises without prejudice to actions by NATO.
>
> (European Council 1999)

The EU possesses sufficient hard power of its member states to project into regions in the near neighbourhood and afar. Its institutional make-up, self-defined role as a civilising power in the world and instruments for external action are indicative of the EU's reluctance towards the use of force in its relations with third parties. Furthermore, member states do not promote collective military strength *per se*. To some extent, member states lack the willingness to cooperate and develop military capabilities (Biscop 2008: 19). While the EU member states are steadily increasing their arms sales to Southeast Asia, sovereignty and domestic concerns impede greater orientation of CSDP towards Southeast Asia.

In spite of this, CSDP will continue to institutionalise and, hence, compel the EU to fulfil the role expectations of a global security actor. Dosch observed that in the context of CSDP, institutions and interests are mutually reinforcing (Dosch 2003). He related the EU's internal developments in that time to the EU's security interest in Southeast Asia and stated,

> The more EU member states harmonised their security interests and the institutionalisation of a Common Foreign and Security Policy took shape, the more the EU developed an interest in discuss[ing] security issues in East Asia.
>
> (Dosch 2003: 494)

The integrative, ideational and geographical settings of the EU largely shape its stance towards Southeast Asian security. The EU as a collective actor does not consider the region as a security priority. CSDP operations have been successful and frequent in the EU's near neighbourhood and Africa, but have been limited to only one mission in Southeast Asia. There appears to be room to make more use of the CSDP experience and resources for peace-keeping, disaster relief or other purposes in the region.

The second EU instrument that holds potential to address a broad range of NTS threats is the RRM, which has now been renamed Instrument for Stability (IfS). The establishment of RRM as a non-political and non-coercive crisis management mechanism followed the European Council meeting in Helsinki on 10 and 11 December 1999. The long-term geographic and thematic instruments in the Asia and Latin America budget line of the European Commission did not have the desired effect. Political crises and conflicts prevented the proper functioning of these instruments. With this in mind, on 26 February 2001, Council Regulation No. 381/2001 was published to set the regulatory framework for RRM until 31 December 2006. This financial mechanism aimed at crisis response and the prevention of emerging conflicts "in a rapid, efficient and flexible manner" (Council of the European Union 2001: 1). It is a short-term instrument complementing the European Commission's thematic, geographic and long-term instruments. RRM allowed the European Commission to act by itself on behalf of the EU and in close coordination with the Council of the EU (Council of the European Union 2001).

Bernd Martenczuk has identified three main advantages of RRM over the other crisis-relevant instruments of the European Commission. Firstly, RRM is more independent because it has its own budget line (Martenczuk 2004: 205). Secondly, it can be applied to a greater number of operations that fall within the European Commission's thematic and geographic instruments (Martenczuk 2004: 205). Thirdly, RRM was designed to avoid time-consuming consultations and decision-making procedures. However, action under this regulation has been limited to six months. This short timeframe was RRM's major operational shortcoming and demanded a re-visit.

On 15 November 2006, Regulation No. 1717/2006 officially replaced RRM with IfS, which provided for engagement of up to 18 months. If required, IfS can be superseded by the Interim Response Measure or extended for another six months depending on the project, budget and whether the objectives still need to be attained (Council of the European Union 2006b: Art. 6.2). Juha Auvinen pointed out that "[c]ompared to the earlier Rapid Reaction Mechanism the crisis response component of the IfS represents a considerable increase in financial allocations (approximately 130 million euro in 2009)" (Auvinen and Wright 2009: 116). In addition to the extended budget, the IfS regulation expands on concrete measures, implementation, and methods of assistance and financing. It expands the EU's collective and international role at the intersection of security and development (European Commission, 28 September 2010: 7). Similarly to the RRM regulation, this instrument acknowledges the security-development nexus and places stronger emphasis on issues of vulnerability and underdevelopment as a cause for insecurity. The measures that can be supported by IfS range from financial, logistical and technical assistance for pre- or post-crisis capacity-building to research on a variety of issues.

On the one hand, IfS appears problematic because its scope of application is wide and may intrude into areas of CSDP competence. On the other hand, one can argue that IfS has been established for the very purpose of creating stable conditions for the CSDP missions to operate in and, thus, is portrayed as complementary to CSDP by the European Commission (European Commission, 28 September 2010). While complementing member state actions, IfS also redefines and strengthens the role of the European Commission as a security actor. This win-win effect is however, ambiguous; since IfS encroaches upon the responsibilities of the member states, although it complements their actions. Despite controversies regarding the functional overlap between the European Commission and the CSDP, IfS enables a more timely response when the European Council cannot achieve a consensus.

IfS is a flexible tool that accommodates both long- and short-term security objectives. It provides for emergency response measures and interim response programmes of up to 18 months. Its long-term component is three-pronged, focusing on non-proliferation of WMD, tackling global and trans-regional threats, and building capacity for effective crisis response. RRM and IfS enhance the speed and scope of the EU's security capability, but, at the same time, they could compromise the EU's core values and principles and tarnish the EU's image as a normative actor. This is a point I will return to in the treatment of the Bali Bombings in Chapter 4.

Politically less controversial is the engagement of the apolitical ECHO unit. ECHO was described earlier on in this book as a key player in the coordination and provision of disaster relief after the Boxing Day Tsunami. ECHO was established in 1992 at the beginning of the worldwide humanitarian intervention debate. Since then, it has provided humanitarian assistance throughout the world. ECHO projects are country-owned and implemented in coordination with international and local partners through community self-help approaches. ECHO has an apolitical, humanitarian and people-oriented mandate. It appears to be a clear-cut tool that frames the EU as a normative actor, in the sense that the EU acts norm-guided and seeks to project norms.

ECHO's engagement in Southeast Asia can be cross-sectoral and long- or short-term. It can involve structural assistance or immediate relief. Below are some examples of ECHO's activities in Southeast Asia:

1. Mainstreaming of disaster risk reduction in the education sector (Lao People's Democratic Republic (PDR), Philippines, and Cambodia)
2. Development of a national disaster risk reduction plan (Cambodia, Philippines, and Vietnam)
3. Development of partnerships, networking, and integration of community-based disaster risk reduction into socio-economic plans at national level (Cambodia, Indonesia, Lao PDR, Philippines, Vietnam, and East Timor).

(European Commission Humanitarian Aid Office 2007)

ECHO can provide assistance through geographic instruments, thematic funding, capacity-building, grants and services, support expenditure, technical assistance and Disaster Preparedness ECHO (DIPECHO). Humanitarian crises caused by natural disasters, including floods, droughts, hazes, earthquakes, landslides and typhoons, have been addressed by the DIPECHO programmes. These programmes were launched in 1996 to provide various forms of assistance in disaster-prone regions. Southeast Asia is one of six regions that have received support from the DIPECHO programmes. So far, a quarter of all the DIPECHO projects worldwide have been conducted in Southeast Asia.

The scope of ECHO support goes beyond natural catastrophes. It also involves medical and food aid, and other forms of aid that alleviate the plight of people after man-made crises. In the context of natural disasters, it is sometimes difficult to distinguish between sudden-onset natural catastrophes and man-made disasters. Often, there is a correlation between the actions of mankind and the circumstances leading to natural disasters. Globalisation and industrialisation have triggered new vulnerabilities, aggravating and complicating the onset and impact of natural disasters. Some examples are environmental degradation, migration to urban centres and new types of plantations that can result in a higher vulnerability to weather phenomena.

Tackling natural disasters in Southeast Asia requires a comprehensive and cross-sectoral response and an understanding of the various correlations between human activity and natural disasters. More specifically, in Southeast Asia, risk reduction can be directly linked to poverty reduction. For this reason, ECHO encourages complementary strategies from other units of the European Commission that address poverty, including the Directorate General for Development or Directorate General for External Relations. This coordination with other units of the European Commission, as well as other state agencies, may heighten the effectiveness of ECHO. However, there is risk too that ECHO may become politicised.

Earlier on in the chapter, I highlighted the politicisation of the EU's development cooperation with Southeast Asia, particularly towards the end of the Cold War and in the early 1990s. The Asia and Latin America regulation was the baseline for the European Commission's development cooperation with Southeast Asia during this time. On 18 December 2006, through Regulation No. 1905/2006, the Development Cooperation Instrument (DCI) was introduced by the European Commission to replace the Asia and Latin America regulation. Since then, it has provided an alternative financial instrument for the European Commission to achieve the Millennium Development Goals (MDGs). DCI is the new legal basis for specific EU–Asia development cooperation and provides long-term financial assistance to developing ASEAN countries. It sets out the geographic, global and thematic programmes according to the following themes: the environment and the sustainable management of natural resources; non-state actors and local authorities; the improvement of food security; and cooperation in the area of migration and asylum.

This instrument contributes to the overall funding of Southeast Asia's regional integration initiatives by the EU. It complements the objectives of the Regional Strategy Paper for EU–Asia Cooperation (2007–2013). Specifically, this instrument is employed to implement "[t]he EU's Multi-annual Indicative Programme [which] has earmarked €40 million to be spent on activities related to EU-ASEAN co-operation from 2007 to 2010" (European Commission 2009). The strategic areas are regional capacity-building and inter-regional dialogue, statistical capacity-building, and immigration and border management. DCI is an important instrument in strengthening inter-regional cooperation and sharing the EU's regional integrative experience.

The preceding paragraphs have demonstrated that the EU has managed to shed its feathers and outgrow the American security architecture of the Cold War period. In a short amount of time, it was able to create a comprehensive toolkit to address emerging security and NTS issues. Through the intergovernmental CSDP, the EU developed military muscle for both civilian and strategic purposes. ECHO and DCI are supranational instruments that link between development and security in the world. They are in essence developmental and humanitarian tools; however, considering the security concerns of some Southeast Asian countries, they ultimately serve the overall security and stability of the region.

This security-development linkage is also applicable to IfS. This tool assists in achieving the long-term development goals of a country and acts as a facilitator for military peace operations. The European Commission's competence has been extended through these instruments to involve the deployment of staff for security purposes. The European Council keeps a close eye on the use of IfS by the European Commission and may thwart IfS activities, if the European Council becomes concerned with competence overlaps.

Conclusions

The preceding paragraphs have provided a discussion of the analytical premises and a historical overview of the ASEAN–EU relationship from an NTS perspective. They have presented the central assumptions of EU security/NTS thinking in relation to Southeast Asia and the main instruments for the EU to address NTS challenges abroad. This chapter has explained that, in a new global security environment, national security is contingent on international security. In this context, the EU and its member states consider their development and humanitarian contributions to Southeast Asia as important avenues to stabilise the region.

This chapter has suggested that the EU is an alternative security actor in the region. Its preference for certain instruments and capabilities, its lack of a strategic presence and its value-laden mind-set make the EU a good mediator and facilitator of partnerships in the region. This chapter has illustrated the avenues and instruments of NTS cooperation, as well as the problems associated with the NTS frame, including the politicisation of development cooperation, the development–security overlap in competencies, and the problem of upholding norms and values against the backdrop of effective cooperation. These issues will be further discussed within the following chapters.

Notes

1 The ASEAN–EC Ministerial Meeting is the main forum in the inter-regional relationship. Since 1995, the ASEAN–EU Senior Officials Meeting has complemented these ministerial meetings. The gathering of the senior officials takes place in between the ministerial meetings and commonly deals with the organisation of these.
2 The European Commission and the ASEAN and EC/EU member states are represented in the JCC by senior officials. The JCC manages the implementation of the Cooperation Agreement of 1980 and consists of five sub-committees that focus on trade and investment, industrial and economic cooperation, science and technology, forestry, environment and narcotics.
3 Translation by author: "jealousy of Africa".

2   The EU and the Asian financial crisis

The AFC was a shock to the economies of East Asia. From June 1997 onwards, the stock markets of the ASEAN member states were melting down and increased capital flight took place. The banking and financial sectors of the ASEAN countries were insufficiently developed and the governments became overstrained with the burden of resolving the crises of the financial markets, the real economy and the human plight. Having experienced three decades of unprecedented growth, many ASEAN states were left unprepared for the risks of the financial markets. Despite incipient attempts to integrate within the financial sector through the intra-regional swap arrangements of 1977, the AFC exposed the need for greater communication and coordination among ASEAN member states. Thai Foreign Minister Surin Pitsuwan even suggested that "ASEAN members perhaps no longer can afford to adopt a non-committal stance and avoid passing judgement on events in a member country, simply on the grounds of 'non-interference'" (Pitsuwan, 1 June 1998).

The AFC led to numerous informal and formal regional meetings. From 1997 onwards the ASEAN Plus Three (APT) process was institutionalised at the third APT Summit in Manila in 1999 to cope with the AFC and other issues of East Asia. By 2000, APT member states had the biggest foreign exchange reserve holdings and, thus, more stability should another regional crisis eventuate. At the APT meeting in Chiang Mai in 2000, the APT members agreed to cooperate on financial matters by information- and data-sharing. Furthermore, a well-coordinated network of contact persons was established for better regional surveillance. The Chiang Mai Initiative was established and provided a cooperative scheme for the monitoring of capital flows, regional surveillance, swap networks and training personnel within East Asia. These arrangements were designed to supplement a member state's foreign exchange reserves, should its currency come under speculative attack. The Chiang Mai Initiative became the point of reference for enhanced

East Asian financial cooperation. It had two components: an expanded ASEAN Swap Arrangement and a network of bilateral swap arrangements among APT member states. It expanded previous ASEAN internal swap arrangements by allowing member states to withdraw double the amount they contributed and to extend the time period.

ASEAN member states recognised that the crisis stemmed from a variety of causes, including currency speculation and volatile and unregulated capital flows, that one single country could not deal with by itself. While the crisis triggered greater regional integration in the financial sector among East Asian countries, it did not necessarily result in a change of the principle of non-interference and the way national sovereignty was perceived. The AFC questioned the utility of these principles; however, ASEAN member states were keen to focus on constructive pathways in enhancing domestic resilience without addressing underlying normative issues.

The main external assistance provider was the International Monetary Fund (IMF). It stepped in as the stabiliser of the international monetary system, assisting the affected Asian countries in containing the AFC. Many Asian states were sceptical about the IMF's involvement. At the Group of 7–IMF Summit of 24–25 September 1997 in Hong Kong, Japan even suggested the creation of an Asian Monetary Fund to resolve the AFC. This controversial proposal was vehemently opposed by the US Treasury and other Western IMF members (Lipscy 2003). One of the G7 representatives involved in the meeting in Manila, where Japan's proposal was dismissed, stated that the overall Asian perception of the IMF was exaggerated and that the objective of the IMF is

> to raise the standard of living and welfare of the IMF member states.... Because the Asians who advocated the Asian Monetary Fund, particularly, the Japanese wanted to avoid IMF conditionality and, in my view and the view of the G7 including the four European countries, conditionality is important when a country gets IMF resources.... The Asian Monetary Fund would have been a way out, avoid conditionality but take money and not fix the problem.
> (Interview with EU official, 18 November 2008)

On the Southeast Asian side, the predominant popular perception was opposed to this position. An Asian scholar said,

> we do not only need to rely on the IMF or World Bank in case of financial turmoil. And during the 1997 financial crisis what ASEAN countries learnt is that the IMF and the World Bank are not really our

friends because they compel the banks to impose some regulation[s] that hurt people.

(interview with Asian think tank representative, 10 November 2008)

Thailand and Indonesia were among the worst-affected ASEAN member states that were supported by the "unloved" IMF packages (interview with Asian think tank representative, 10 November 2008). These rescue packages comprised funds and loans linked to conditionality. Thailand and Indonesia also experienced significant political instabilities following the outbreak of the crisis. In both countries, the AFC enhanced political cleavages among the political elite. The devaluation of the currency and the rising prices of commodities in Indonesia led to demonstrations, violent clashes and rampages by anti-Suharto protesters, resulting in hundreds of deaths in Jakarta. In Thailand, the damage by the AFC also hit the political arena and obliged Prime Minister Chaovalit Yongchaiyudh to resign from his position. Both the state and society were the victims and, therefore, the security referents of the crisis.

The AFC has been analysed in numerous ASEAN–EU studies and discussions (Council for Asia–Europe Cooperation 2000; Lee 2000; Langhammer 2001; Robles Jr. 2004). Even today, both European and East Asian scholars still disagree on whether it showed the EU's true colours of a fair-weather friend which is there only when it can benefit from the relationship. These accusations still echo in the heads of some Asians, who seem unaware that there were EU member states which were indeed concerned when the AFC broke out. The unfolding of the crisis showed that Asia's problem affected Europe in many ways.

Evidently, there was a degree of *Schadenfreude* on the European side that the Asian Miracle was no longer miraculous (Higgott 1998). However, Europe's glee was short-lived. Firstly, there were fears that the outbreak was contagious and could impact the European financial markets. Secondly, there were fears that the loans given to some Asian states might never be paid back. In light of these realities, how was the issue of contagion perceived and framed? The EU began to fear the spread of the AFC in light of the continual reporting of Japanese bank failures, in particular. The rising interest rates and the downturn of the stocks in Moscow in mid-January of 1998 also contributed to the growing concerns of many European financial experts. These experts were concerned that the crisis could become a global crisis. This fear was not shared equally across Western Europe. For example, in January 1998, the European Commission President, Jacques Santer, downplayed the impact of the AFC on the EU (Bridges 1999; Robles Jr. 2008). In June 1998, Germany's

Minister of Economic Affairs, Günter Rexrodt, defused speculations of a global financial crash. He expressed his faith in the IMF and said that the situation was under control (Follath and Wagner 22, June 1998). By contrast, the chief economist of the Deutsche Bank, Norbert Walter, warned that the West had so far underestimated the AFC (Follath and Wagner, 22 June 1998).

In fact, European exporters were already feeling the pressure. The employment rates decreased and the profit of many of the European exporting companies sunk. Once the yen fell below its lowest point of the past seven years, the reactions rapidly changed to become more negative across the EU. At the European Council meeting of 15–16 June 1998 in Cardiff, the AFC was an important topic. It was discussed as a threat to the European markets which needed close monitoring. This was necessary in order to protect the European economies, as well as to ensure the successful introduction of the euro on 1 January 1999 (Presidency of the European Council 1998). At the meeting, the host, Tony Blair, even spoke of the AFC as the greatest threat for the global economy in the last 20 years (Blustein and Richburg, 16 June 1998).

The EU's perceptions of the crisis and its assistance to Southeast Asia were dependent on the degree of interdependence and contagion. Prior to the AFC, the EU constructed the image of Asia as the greatest opportunity for European investors and companies. Germany was among the investors who supported this image and loaned approximately DM[1] 16 billion to Indonesia. During the AFC, Germany actively engaged in diplomacy with Indonesia to recover some of its loans. Despite great concerns about the repayment of the loans, Germany continued with technical assistance in the financial sector (interview with EU official, 18 November 2008). Germany's overall long-term assistance to Indonesia did not depend on the issue of the loans. This indicates that many areas of cooperation function independent from each other. Short-term and crisis-dependent cost-benefit calculations cannot thwart decade-old development cooperation.

Amid the AFC, development cooperation did not cease, but the idea that Asia was an investment opportunity evaporated. The EU was relieved that not many companies had followed its 'Go East' slogan. It supported the IMF in containing the spread, although some EU members criticised the IMF and called for a new Bretton Woods system (Siemens, 14 November 2008). In the beginning of the crisis, the AFC was perceived as a threat only by some European political and business elites. With greater unfolding of the crisis, European leaders became more concerned. It was understood across Europe that the EU needed to act to safeguard its economy.

The trade and investment pledge and other initiatives

The AFC was a socio-economic threat for the EU and, therefore, the EU member states provided substantial material help. As Julie Gilson described,

> Governmental attempts were made to address a number of problems resulting from the crisis. The EU pledged bilaterally US$5.9 billion to the Republic of Korea's second line of defence (compared with US$10 billion from Japan and $5 billion from the US), in addition to the bilateral technical assistance offered by some EU member states. Meanwhile, private European banks also rolled over some of their short-term credits. On one side, Asian participants recognised the need for European investment and funds to help [t]rade relations between Europe and East Asia redress the economic chaos and to keep European markets open to Asian goods…. On the other, the EU recognised long-term benefits in aiding the Asian recovery. Since Asian borrowers were still paying off the estimated US$365 billion they owed to European banks (as of June 1997, and compared with US$275 billion for Japan and US$45 billion for the US), there was a need to recoup European investment.
>
> (Gilson 2004: 193–194)

Gilson describes the cost-benefit calculations behind the EU's actions. The trade barriers were not raised and large amounts of financial assistance were made available by individual EU member states. This financial support was mostly channelled to Southeast Asia and Northeast Asia under the auspices of the IMF. The EU member states allocated approximately US$154 million in total to the international financial institutions (Brittan 1999: 492). This amount was second to Japan's contribution of about 20 per cent of the total budget.

In the dialogue framework of ASEM, the ASEM Asia Financial Crisis Response Trust Fund or, in brief, the ASEM Trust Fund (ATF) and the European Financial Expertise Network (EFEX) were structures created at ASEM 2 in response to the AFC. The ATF was administered by the World Bank. The EU and the World Bank placed importance on country ownership and met with the recipients on a regular six-month basis to design country-tailored programmes. The ATF started in the summer of 1998 with ATF 1 to provide help for immediate social and financial recovery. ATF 1 closed at the end of 2002 and gave way to ATF 2. The latter was long-term oriented and phased out in 2006. ATF 1 had a total of US$47.5 million at its disposal and this amount was disbursed to 71 projects in Indonesia, Thailand, Vietnam, Malaysia and the Philippines (World Bank 2003: ii). South Korea and China also received benefits from this scheme. Beyond the country programmes, ATF 1 also included eight multi-country or regional approaches that totalled US$4.7 million (World Bank 2003: viii). Five of these projects aimed to help the social sector. The other three were designed to aid the financial and corporate sector. The AFC affected the ASEAN member states differently. Thus, the inter-regional approach was a secondary means mainly aimed at strengthening the regional integrative dynamics.

The EU rated the projects as a success, because they met the "initial objectives, [produced] a substantial body of materials and [conducted] important learning workshops" (World Bank 2003: 26). Noteworthy is the role of the regional programmes, which strengthened the role of the ASEAN Secretariat through workshops and best practice sharing. Among these projects was the project Forming Shared Regional Views on Economic Prospects (TF022371), which looked at regional information sharing and development analyses to advocate a greater role for the ASEAN Secretariat in regional monitoring and surveillance. With this project, ASEAN started to consider creating a permanent monitoring and policy review facility within the Secretariat (World Bank 2003: 27). Southeast Asia was given merely seven regional projects and the allocated amount to the regional projects was comparatively minimal, as shown in Figures 2.1 and 2.2. While the AFC was the main catalyst for regional integration in this area, the regional projects supported by the ATF acted as additional stimuli.

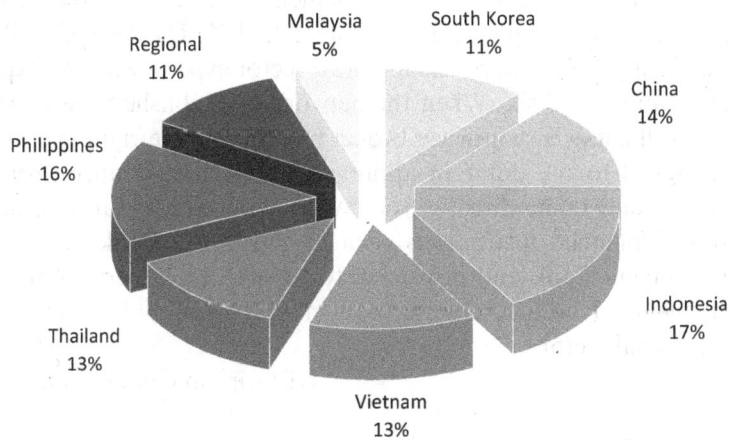

Figure 2.1 ATF 1 recipients
Data Source: Asian Financial Crisis Response Fund 1 Completion Report (2003)

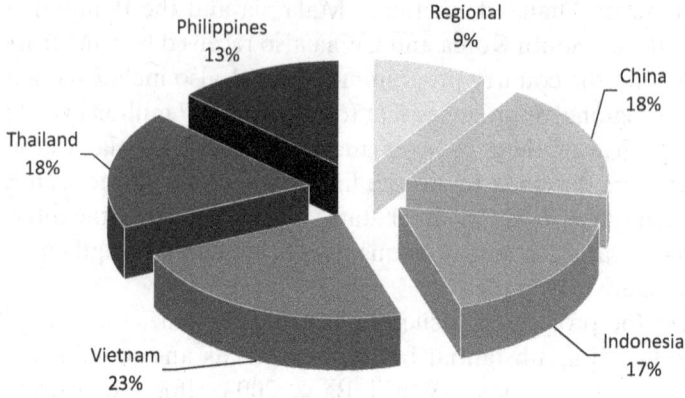

Figure 2.2 ATF 2 recipients
Data Source: Financial Crisis Response Trust Fund Report 2 (2007)

The European Commission also initiated EFEX to provide a network and database of European and Asian financial experts who can be consulted and employed for the implementation of projects concerning the AFC. This initiative was adopted at ASEM 2 and was put under the responsibility of DG Markt. It became fully operational in January 1999, but lacked interest and phased out shortly after. The following European Commission communication describes the purpose of EFEX.

> The main objective of this network is to increase both the quantity and quality of advice provided by European experts to Asian countries seeking to restructure their financial sector. The Commission has set up a "clearing house" to manage EFEX. The network will be open to all private and public financial sector experts with the experience required in Asia. When the network is established the clearing house will act as a "marriage broker" by finding the right experts to be assigned to the different approved technical assistance projects. Requests may come directly from Asian countries or through international financial institutions such as the World Bank and Asian Development Bank and private sector operators. Experts should be available to advise their counterparts in Asia on all topics relevant for the financial sector.
>
> (European Commission 1998)

Southeast Asian countries were reluctant to draw upon foreign expertise overly in restructuring the financial sector. EFEX maintained the donor-recipient asymmetry of the ASEAN–EU relationship and lacked appeal to a region already deeply suspicious of foreign assistance.

The third response launched by the ASEM members at the London Summit was the ASEM Trade and Investment Pledge. This pledge was to assure that the ASEM participants would not succumb to protectionist measures and keep their markets open. Former Vice-President Sir Leon Brittan of the European Commission even claimed that this inter-regional pledge "set the tone for the response of other fora to the crisis – for example, in the G7 and the [World Trade Organisation (WTO)]" (Brittan 1999: 492). ASEM participants are also members of other international fora, where they meet and refer to ASEM discussions. ASEM's role in coordinating a common stance on the AFC was important and helped facilitate the later discussions on the higher multilateral plains. However, Brittan's claim of ASEM being an active vehicle in shaping and streamlining the issue-specific discourse on the international level lacks clear evidence.

To measure up to the pledge, the second ASEM Summit initiated the Trade Facilitation Action Plan (TFAP) and the Investment Promotion Action Plan (IPAP). These aimed at deepening the inter-regional economic and financial cooperation. They were designed to reduce trade barriers and promote investment. These institutional innovations have been the umbrella for a multitude of trade- and investment-related seminars and working groups, including the Investment Experts Group or the Working Group on Sanitary and Phytosanitary Measures. Despite the pledge, the foreign direct investment (FDI) figures between the two sides shrunk in the following two years, before they regained volume. Julie Gilson observed,

> While both of these initiatives [TFAP and IPAP] were intended to offer a flagship policy for ASEM, they, too, have suffered from the broader problem of sustaining interest among participants of the ASEM process as a whole. This is in part due to the ways in which business activities function independently of regional and political structures, and in part due to the very loose framework of ASEM, which imposes no strict regime of accountability.
>
> (Gilson 2004: 190–191)

Gilson blamed ASEM's soft institutions and the dynamic inherent in the Asia–Europe trade relations as the spoilers of the inter-regional momentum. On a different note, Southeast Asia was not interested in a solution that was primarily designed by Europeans and aimed at upholding European economic interests, although Southeast Asian interests were accounted for through TFAP and IPAP to some extent. Similarly to EFEX, TFAP and IPAP failed to sustain Asian interests. Even if stronger institutions were created, this may not necessarily increase the contingency between business activities and ASEM structures. As Gilson indicated, the solution could lie in the creation of a free trade regime linked to the ASEM process.

This pledge confirmed Southeast Asia's suspicion about the EU's economic motivations to some extent. The EU and its member states benefited from the pledge in the sense that Southeast Asia did not resort to protectionist measures and continued with market liberalisation (Kerr et al. 1999). William Kerr and colleagues believed that the EU and its member states employed altruist rhetoric to frame their materialistic intentions. They stated that by 1998, the EU increasingly realised that ASEM could serve as a vehicle for gaining better access to Asian markets (Kerr et al. 1999: 74). The pledge packaged interests in a normative frame to help push trade and facilitate the recovery. In this light, the pledge can be considered as an instrument of political strategy to further EU influence.

The initiatives supported by the EU were in practice less intrusive than the loans of the IMF. From a Southeast Asian perspective, the international funds linked to the conditionality of the IMF loans provided an opportunity for the West to harness Southeast Asia's economic potential. They aimed at "restructuring" the financial sector of some Southeast Asian countries (interview with Asian think tank representative 10 November 2008). The EU and its member states did not have the institutional mechanisms of the IMF to enforce the recovery of loans. This demonstrates that solidarity is not the only calculus; self-protection and -preservation are closely linked notions driving EU interaction with Southeast Asia. For international political actors, it appears that sometimes expressions of solidarity are a method for framing economic objectives. Interests and normative goals are intertwined and frequently used instrumentally to reinforce each other. This partially contradicts the initial assumption of the book that the ASEAN–EU relationship is shaped by the ideational dimension.

The EU and its member states have formulated and developed a variety of responses to assist Southeast Asia in the aftermath of the AFC. The EU has been a significant financial donor. It and its member states have channelled a high amount of funds through the IMF and other institutions. Through ATF 1 and 2, the EU managed to develop inter-regional projects supporting regional integration in East Asia. The AFC has triggered enhanced EU support to Southeast Asia. However, at the same time, the AFC has crystallised Southeast Asia's vulnerabilities and the need for the EU to pay greater attention to the region in light of the ever-growing interdependence.

Interdependence complicates the identification of clear-cut motivations of the international actors. It can shed both bad and good lights on the actors. Immediately, when the AFC broke out, some European leaders were concerned about the degree of contagion and the economic impact on Europe. Other political and business elites did not fear the AFC. The AFC appeared localised to Southeast Asia and, thus, initially the EU and its member states seemed unaffected and less alarmed. In light of this low degree of threat perception, the EU's and its member states' immediate assistance through the IMF appeared to be norm-guided. Being multilateralist by definition, the EU seeks to uphold international institutions and comply with its commitments within them. At the same time, the EU acted on the basis of its economic interests. Once leaders realised the impact of the AFC on the European economies, various mechanisms to protect European interests were activated. The pledge was conceived and many European governments became concerned about retrieving their loans.

The role of the ASEM Finance Ministers' Meeting

The AFC gave ASEM and, specifically, the ASEM Finance Ministers' Meeting (ASEM FinMM) a limelight position in enhancing the EU's profile as an actor in Southeast Asia. The ASEAN–EU dialogue had reached an impasse on Myanmar's accession. ASEM provided an alternative avenue to continue with the official dialogue of the two sides and, specifically, the ASEM FinMMs allowed both sides to delve into the technical aspects of the AFC and its management.

The ASEM FinMM process was launched prior to the AFC. In the first meeting, it was "agreed that it would be useful to schedule meetings of ASEM Finance Deputies to discuss international financial issues raised in other monetary and financial fora" (ASEM Finance Ministers 1997: para. 18). In the aftermath of the AFC, ASEM FinMM assumed greater pertinence. It benefitted from the cooperative dynamic during the crisis. Whereas the first ASEM FinMM emulated the agenda of other global fora, the subsequent meetings were moulded by the AFC and the volatile dynamics of the financial markets. The ASEM FinMMs discussed a broad range of issues, including the volatility of oil prices, the World Trade Organisation and the tackling of money laundering.

The AFC was mainly discussed at the second ASEM FinMM on 15 February 1999. At this meeting, Japan and China committed to concrete efforts and declared they would provide substantial financial support in assisting the crisis-affected states in the region. The participating finance ministers "agreed to deepen the exchange of views amongst ASEM partners concerning the international financial architecture", among other commitments (ASEM Finance Ministers 1999: para. 7). ASEM FinMM also initiated long-term projects for financial development, including the ASEM Public Debt Management Forum, the Kobe Research Project[2] (both in 2001), the Bali Initiative, the Symposium on Combating Underground Banking and Supervising Alternate Remittance Systems (both in 2003) and the Tianjin Initiative on Closer Economic and Financial Cooperation.

The Tianjin Initiative acknowledged the various dialogue-based efforts and called for a stronger action-oriented focus of the forum. It specifically addressed the creation of the ASEM YES (Yen-Euro-Dollar) Bond Market and the ASEM Bond Fund. The Tianjin Initiative also called for the establishment of the ASEM Contingency Dialogue Mechanism for Emergent Economic and Financial Events to address the financial and economic insecurity after natural disasters.

This mechanism supports the relief and reconstruction efforts and allows a timely launch of these. It progressively links between different sectors of governance and remedies the ASEM FinMMs lack of cross-sectoral activities. This is important when addressing crises in their entirety and provides an avenue for tangible cooperation to spill over into other areas. However, this mechanism represents an emergency measure that should not whitewash bad governance. It is only effective if it goes hand in hand with existing development cooperation and reforms in the financial sector. It needs to address financial standards within other sectors of governance. In the context of Southeast Asia, this includes the systematic decentralisation of auditing and distributive elements to attain sustainable economies.

The majority of the measures advanced by the ASEM FinMMs are designed to build confidence and facilitate an exchange of information. At the same time, European Commission officials have indicated that this inter-regional dialogue could serve as a clearing house layer for other international fora (interview with EU official, 9 February 2009). A European Commission official expands on this thought and exemplifies the case of the quota misrepresentation of the emerging economies and some other states in the Bretton Woods system.

> The IMF had two years to reform the quota system. Within the IMF the members met every six months, but they could not reach an agreement. So, by September 2006, after two years, they had to find a consensus and they finally managed to do so. This was mainly because half of the world met within the ASEM framework from 8–9 April 2006 and had this additional opportunity to exchange views on the problem.
> (interview with EU official, 9 February 2009)

The consensus was not necessarily found within the ASEM framework since the "so-called other part of the world was missing" (interview with EU official, 9 February 2009). Nevertheless, it facilitated the consensus-building process on the international level, since the two big groups of players of the Bretton Woods system had already discussed and provided a basis for the agreement at the IMF.

The ASEM FinMM dialogue is also a learning experience for both sides, although the EU's practices are considered as the benchmark (interview with EU official, 9 February 2009). The Asian side takes a completely different approach to regional economic and financial integration and thus, "it is also quite interesting for the European side to hear" the Southeast Asian perspective (interview with EU official, 9 February 2009). This "learning" by the Europeans is not necessarily "about what the Asian side is doing, as this is limited" and the dialogue partners are usually informed about each other's measures (interview with EU official, 9 February 2009). It is rather "a little bit knowing about the new measures and what they have got in the pipeline...and then it is learning why they are not doing more, what their concerns are and what they aim to achieve realistically" (interview in Maier-Knapp 2014: 226). This suggests that ASEM itself is a mechanism to improve better understanding between the counterparts.

When the EU shares its experience or gives advice, it is also attempting to move Asian integration towards a direction it likes and that serves Europe (interview in Maier-Knapp 2014: 226). The European Commission official further explained,

> I think so in a way. It is not so much about defending Europe [but] trying to shape what is going on at the global level in a way that is either more favourable, but also already underway in Europe [and] convincing Asia through ASEM that what Europe is doing is good.
> (interview in Maier-Knapp 2014: 226)

This is evidence of the EU's normative agenda and indicates the extent to which the EU intertwines its economic and political interests in Asia with an ideational/ethical dimension. Even within putatively technical sectors of cooperation, the EU will try to frame its actions along normative lines (Maier-Knapp 2014: 227). The question here is whether a matter that is 'good' for everyone necessarily needs to be accepted as 'good' by the EU's partners (interview with EU official, 9 February 2009). This aspect is very important, since it highlights that even in the financial sector, which is very technical and less value-laden, there are ideological and structural differences. For example, the different types of working cultures of the national bureaucracies within Asia also complicate coordination and communication within Asia, as well as with Europe (interview with EU official, 9 February 2009).

Overall, the European Commission official's words suggest that, within the ASEM FinMMs, the EU is driven by both norms and interests. In her view, the ASEM FinMM dialogue and cooperation needs to be seen as a means to create lasting structures that are conducive to greater EU influence in East Asia. Based on the ASEM FinMM agenda, the guiding motivations of action display a strong cost-benefit rationale that shows normative traces when framed by the EU. By contrast, the proposals on the Southeast Asian side, including the Public-Private Partnerships, mainly aim at extracting financial support from the EU (interview with EU official, 9 February 2009).

The EU seeks to spread its norms and values and, at the same time, bring the Asian side into a constructive dialogue on economic and financial matters that can interest both sides. "While on our side, while we wanted cooperation. Cooperation in terms of, as we said, when we want to try that when we meet on the global level they are on our side and not on the US side.... So it is less material[istic]" (interview with EU official, 9 February 2009). While both sides take interest in the content of the discussion, the Southeast Asian side seems to have more interest in the tangible wealth of the richer dialogue partner (interview with EU official, 9 February 2009). From a European perspective, the dialogue itself is valuable and considered as an end goal.

This putative difference in objectives, normative motivations and contexts has also been observed by a former Director-General for Economic and Financial Affairs, who said that, "[t]here are differences in how Asians and Europeans address certain problems. Asians want to prepare very well and they are not very spontaneous as we know, except in the nightlife in Singapore" (interview with EU official, 18 November 2008). He added, "I don't think one can say that the Europeans want to talk about a certain range of topics and the Asians want to talk about a certain range of topics" (interview with EU official, 18 November 2008). Talks are driven by "country-based interests" and the ideological split between Europe and Asia is not clear-cut (interview with EU official, 18 November 2008). He argued that the ASEM FinMMs reflect a broad agenda ranging from climate change to counter-terrorism and that while these topics have financial and normative implications, they are primarily an issue of enforcement. They do not clearly point to an ideological divide between Asia and Europe.

He explained that "on counter-terrorism there might be a more systemic split; if there were weaknesses in enforcements of anti-money-laundering, it was probably mainly on the Asian side" (interview with

EU official, 18 November 2008). He said that when the EU enlarged and weaker countries joined, systemic problems revolving around enforcement also became apparent on the European side. The extent to which the ideational dimension is drawn upon in the activities of an international actor is highly dependent on the systemic reality of the individual countries and regions. In his opinion, the different interests and actions stem from the divergence in development as well as the availability of resources and capacities. European ASEM FinMM participants understand the difference in approach and the technical nature of the sector, which inhibits the explicit promotion of the core norms and values within this dialogue format.

Response within the ASEAN–EU dialogue and the ARF

So far, the chapter has displayed ASEM as the prominent channel of communication during the AFC. The ASEAN–EU Ministerial Meeting and JCCs were postponed, because of Myanmar's accession in 1997. The official communication was suspended and resumed at the ASEAN–EU Ministerial Meeting in Vientiane of 11–12 December 2000. The joint declaration of Vientiane stated,

> We welcomed the successful launch of the Euro in 1999, as well as the economic recovery that had taken place in ASEAN. We agreed on the importance of continued economic and financial reforms at the national level, and of global cooperation in the reform of the international financial architecture, for sustainable economic recovery and the prevention of a recurrence of the crisis. We recognised the economic dynamism of the two regional groupings and agreed that this reinforced the rationale for enhanced cooperation in all fields.
> (ASEAN and EU member states 2000: para. 16)

This meeting did not come up with concrete plans of cooperation and assistance. However, it was a positive signal that promised "enhanced cooperation in all fields" (ASEAN and EU member states 2000: para. 16). The meeting was held well after the lowpoint of the AFC, but, nevertheless, it showed European solidarity towards the grave situation in Southeast Asia.

Similarly to the rhetoric within the ASEM framework, the various ASEAN–EU Ministerial Meeting declarations suggest that the EU was interested to see Southeast Asia continue liberalising in trade and investment in order for Europe to uphold its market interests. Within the JCC, the joint response from 1999 stated,

> Both sides agreed to work together to meet the challenges raised by the recent economic crisis faced by ASEAN. The European side expressed its support to the ASEAN countries affected by the crisis, and was confident that ASEAN would emerge stronger from its present difficulties. In this respect, the [Commission] stated its willingness to maintain its contribution in the region to support ASEAN's efforts in its economic recovery process. The [Commission] suggested priority actions on trade, investment and economic restructuring in response to the crisis. Both sides reaffirmed their commitments to further trade and investment liberalisation and to the multilateral trading system, and their determination to fight any protectionist pressures, which might arise from the crisis. The JCC stressed the importance of the European continued support and assistance for ASEAN to effectively deal with the economic and financial crisis
>
> (ASEAN member countries and European Commission 1999: para. 3)

Overall, within the ASEAN–EU dialogue, the European engagement remained primarily declaratory and focused on highlighting that there is no need for protectionism. After the fall-out over Myanmar, the EU resorted to a soft-spoken and declaratory stance on the AFC. It seemed to be a fair-weather friend concerned with protecting the European economies. That is, in the aftermath of the AFC, the ASEAN–EU dialogue has been used as a platform for economic sweet-talk. This symbolic interaction has been important to overcome the strained relationship. Within low-profile institutional frameworks, mutual trust and confidence are important in facilitating cooperation, particularly after a phase of silence or miscommunication.

Within the ARF framework, the AFC was considered an important security concern. It acted as a catalyst to strengthen the role of the ARF as a safeguard for regional stability. The EU as one of many dialogue partners within the ARF supported this view.

> The Ministers discussed extensively the prevailing financial situation in the region. They were encouraged by initial signs of progress towards financial stability in the Asian region. The Ministers welcomed the various individual, bilateral, regional and multilateral measures that were undertaken to restore financial stability. [...] [T]he Mi[ni]sters called for a balanced approach in addressing the socioeconomic impact of such reforms, particularly its impact on the less privileged sectors of society. They noted that certain aspects of the regional financial crisis could impact on the peace and security of

the region and agreed that the ARF would have an important role to play in addressing these effects. The Ministers agreed that the current Asian economic difficulties should not undermine the process of ARF and other regional security dialogues and cooperation.

(ARF member countries 1998: para. 11–12)

The preceding paragraphs suggested the EU as an actor in relation to the AFC mainly within the frameworks of the IMF and ASEM. The ASEAN–EU relationship and the ARF did not provide significant evidence beyond the declaratory level. This added to the EU's invisible profile during the AFC years, although the EU as a whole offered significant financial support to Asia through various channels. It appears that the overall Southeast Asian perception was that the IMF and the USA were the main actors. In the end, this proved to be useful for the EU to some extent, since the IMF's conditional assistance was perceived negatively by the East Asian side. The conditionality of the IMF loans generated an increased distrust towards the USA and the Bretton Woods system. The overall perceptions of the IMF and general Western assistance were viewed critically.

By definition, the EU and its member states do not undermine the international institutions and benefit from the administrative burden-sharing (Maier-Knapp 2010: 84, 95). Although funds passed on to multilateral international donors may alleviate the EU's workload, a recent study by Stephen Booth and Siân Herbert suggested that this practice may actually decrease the EU's aid effectiveness (Booth and Herbert 2011). They speak of a "wasteful chain of transfers" and state that EU funds may be recycled up to three times among donors; this means additional administrative costs at each stage before they reach the recipients (Booth and Herbert 2011: 12, 13).

The IMF is the appropriate multilateral financial institution to manage a global crisis in this sector. The EU is not interested in duplicating efforts and competing with the IMF, of which the EU states are members. When assistance is executed by an international institution with a set of issue-specific international standards, this appears to be a more effective method. It circumvents the quarrels with third parties over the conditions of the implementation of the funds.

The EU and its member states behave as committed members to multilateral fora, because this also strengthens the EU's international legitimacy. However, channelling financial assistance through the international institutions decreases the EU's visibility as an actor to some extent. The sociological 'other' cannot perceive the EU as an actor, unless the IMF and other international institutions clearly flag the origin of the financial contributions. There is an asymmetry in contribution and recognition. The EU is a payer, but rarely appears, or is rarely perceived, as an actor.

Beyond the financial contributions, the EU and its member states distinguished themselves as expertise providers in the various seminars and initiatives related to the ASEM framework. Within ASEM, both the European Commission and the individual member states were active in proposing projects that mainly targeted the long-term dimension to improve financial practices. Both sides were keen to create greater confidence. Notwithstanding, the EU failed to enter into a constructive dialogue with the ASEAN side on reforming the Bretton Woods system and missed out on the possibility of mobilising ASEAN and Asian sympathies to push its interests against the USA in the WTO and other multilateral fora.

Generally speaking, when the EU has had disagreements on financial and economic issues that were resolved in the various multilateral fora, the EU lacked allies against the USA. An EU official explained,

> One example is, you may have heard about fair-value accounting.... When this was negotiated the Europeans tried to stop that and we lost against the Americans. [...] if the Asians had been more outspoken, more involved in drawing this regulation, they also dislike short-termism, we could have won the argument maybe against the Americans [...]. It is not that we want to be anti-American, it is just natural for Europeans and for Asians to have a more longer term view. How that can be helpful than to make certain recommendations even before it gets to the question that you have more or less. Even those that you have can be more longer-term oriented or shorter-term oriented and there I think we should be great partners, the Asians and the Europeans.... The objective is not to isolate or criticise or fingerpoint at the US. That is not the objective. But I think it could be a productive objective to just discover that Asia and Europe have many things in common [...]. [The Americans] will have a very important voice, they are the biggest economy in the world. But if Asia and Europe are convinced that their instincts are better in certain aspects they will have a good chance to outvote the US better than before.
>
> (interview with EU official, 18 November 2008)

This observation illustrates the American dominance of the international financial system. At the same time, it demonstrates European interests in coalescing with Asia in various international economic and financial institutions. The AFC has been a missed opportunity for the Europeans to assist the Southeast Asian side in demanding a reform of the Bretton Woods system. The AFC was not a grave concern for the EU, and thus it did not mobilise anti-Bretton Woods sentiments on the European side. Furthermore, it is understood that the main player of the game will "be more equal" than others and that the EU also shares a high degree of ideological commonality on international financial markets with the USA and has to carefully balance its interests (interview with EU official, 18 November 2008).

Conclusions

This chapter has shown that the AFC marked the beginning of the debate on NTS threats and issue-specific forms of regional integration within ASEAN, as well as within the ASEAN–EU dialogue from 1999 onwards. It illustrated that the EU and its member states varied in their interpretation of the AFC. Some European leaders, including Tony Blair, portrayed the AFC as a major threat, however, securitisation of the AFC remained limited from a European perspective. The EU as a whole was interested in assisting, and was guided by both normative and cost-benefit rationales. Furthermore, it was suggested that the AFC was an incident that allowed the EU to promote measures that could further its economic and trade interests with the Southeast Asian region.

The AFC enhanced the interaction between the two regions. It offered an opportunity for the EU to share its regional integrative experience with ASEAN and launch a variety of inter-regional programmes. However, these inter-regional initiatives remained restricted from the outset. This was mainly because of the temporally and spatially uneven affectedness of the ASEAN states. Additionally, the ASEAN Secretariat did not possess the capacity to manage many initiatives. The EU's overall engagement complemented the national recovery of Southeast Asian states.

The AFC highlighted the vulnerabilities of Southeast Asia as a developing region. It showed to the EU that regions far away from Europe can be a source of insecurity for Europe and that the EU and its member states need to pay closer attention to Southeast Asia. While the AFC did raise European awareness of Southeast Asia in political terms, it did not encourage the EU and its member states to adopt a NTS perspective on financial activities and markets. The AFC was not a crisis to Europe. Overall, its impact on Europe was limited and did not necessitate the EU and its member states to significantly innovate and alter domestic policies to improve their own resilience.

Notes

1 Deutschemark.
2 At the third ASEM FinMM the Kobe Research Project was adopted. It aimed to facilitate inter-regional research cooperation on macroeconomic and financial issues through knowledge collaboration, exchange, analysis and collection of information gained through regional experiences; by creating a network of expertise among ASEM policymakers and think tanks; and by making policy suggestions to the ASEM Track I members. Similarly to ATF 2, this project belongs to an inter-regional response to the AFC targeting the long-term and sustainable development of the financial sector. It is an inter-regional initiative of the second phase, after the first phase, consisting of fire-fighting responses, has been completed.The goal of the initiatives of the second phase is to sustain the post-crisis development through reforms. The Kobe Research Project comprises research projects conducted by the Asian Development Bank, the IMF, the European Central Bank and individual ASEM member states under the following headings: Exchange Rate Regimes for Emerging East Asian and EU Accession Countries, Currency regimes: The European Experience and Implication for East Asia, Strengthening Financial Cooperation and Surveillance, Enhancing Regional Monitoring and Integration: Instruments, Steps, and Sequencing, The European and Asian Financial Systems in Perspective: The Cases of Spain and China, China in a Regional Monetary Framework, and Banking Sector Reform and Capital Market Development. These national and regional case studies serve to show best practices that can be introduced to avoid certain problems from occurring or recurring.Although the project is designed to be a platform for sharing research results and experience, it is suspiciously dominated by pro-regional integration jargon on the European side. The research papers that were presented stressed the success of the European monetary and financial integration on the one hand. On the other hand, they also advised East Asia to learn from the European experience and adopt best practices from international declarations, including the Basel Core Principles.

3 The EU and the haze

Parallel to the devastating unfolding of the AFC, a smoke blanket, the so-called haze, stemming from the land and forest fires in Indonesia, also severely impacted the Southeast Asian economies. Peter Waldman reported in 1997,

> This season's Indonesian fires, like the Southeast Asian currency crisis before them, have forced a rare moment of truth on a region more accustomed to flattery. Suddenly, evidence of serious economic and environmental disorders in several booming Southeast Asian countries has been laid bare.
>
> (Waldman 1997)

The year 1997 was incisive for Southeast Asia, experiencing transboundary challenges that questioned the extent to which the states and the region as a whole were prepared for managing contemporary risks and challenges. The rapid growth of the economies opened up new sites of vulnerability that received marginal attention from within, as well as without the region. In spite of some external assistance on the haze issue during the Cold War period, it was not until 1997 that this extreme case of the haze led to greater regional integrative dynamics and external assistance.

This chapter elaborates on the activities of the EU and its member states in assisting Indonesia and Southeast Asia with the haze problem. While the EU did and does not perceive the haze stemming from Indonesia as a threat, it understands that the haze has a severe impact on Southeast Asian economies and regional integrative processes. In addition to this, the EU is also driven by the European public, which is interested in environmental protection and curbing illegal logging as well as illegal timber trade from the region.

The discussion begins with an outline of the impact of the haze, before shedding light on ASEAN's regional response to this problem and the extent to which the EU assisted in managing this issue. It places particular

52 *The EU and the haze*

focus on European engagement in the case of the haze in 1997. Overall, the chapter seeks to deliver to the research questions and establish the central characteristics of the EU's engagement on this issue. It further discusses issues of forest governance related to the haze, since good and sustainable forest governance can help mitigate the haze problem.

The haze and ASEAN regional integrative dynamics

The land and forest fires recur on an annual basis and are common to the Southeast Asian region. They are caused by an interplay of climatic phenomena (El Niño Southern Oscillation in the case of Indonesia), and socio-economic and institutional factors. The main causes for the smoke or haze resulting from these fires have been associated with traditional agricultural practices of slash and burn. Trade globalisation has amplified the need to burn land for profit. The haze has impacted the welfare and activities of Southeast Asian peoples and states significantly (Dennis 1999; Sastry 2002). Over the years, the haze has affected Malaysia, Indonesia, Brunei, Singapore and, to a lesser extent, Thailand and the Philippines.

The smoke from the fires in Indonesia is particularly extensive and sometimes spreads to neighbouring countries. In Indonesia, burning land is illegal, but so far punitive measurements by the Government of Indonesia (GoI) have not halted this trend and it is suggested that the emphasis needs to be placed on the rule of law. Despite the annual recurrence of the haze for over two decades, law enforcement remains weak. It was not until 1997 that the GoI actually started penalising large companies for their devastating role in the fires of that year (Dennis 1999: 14–15).

In 1997, the haze from the fires was particularly severe. Studies estimated the economic and social costs to be US$3–6 billion. The ASEAN Response Strategy document of 2001 stated that the 1997–1998 haze period caused an economic loss, excluding social and environmental costs, estimated to be about US$6 billion and a spatial distribution of 8 million ha for Indonesia (ASEAN and Asian Development Bank researchers 2001: xv). Rona Dennis estimated the following losses resulting from the fire and haze: for Indonesia, US$3.8 billion, and for the neighbouring ASEAN members, US$0.7 billion (Dennis 1999: 16). In Indonesia alone "an estimated 20–70 million people suffered health problems [...] and 40,000 people were hospitalised" (Timmer 2000: 9).

The tables below give a general idea of the devastation caused by the fires of 1997 in Indonesia. They include spatial and financial assessments, the area burnt, pollution, impact on human health and economic suffering. Similarly to the AFC, both the state and the people were the security

Table 3.1 Forest status and burnt area

Forest status	Total area burnt (ha)
Protection forest	21,963
Production forest	163,444
Nature reserves and wildlife sanctuaries	17,238
Recreation forest	1,415
National parks	54,331
Grand forest park	653
Research forest	4,741
Urban forest	5
Hunting park	202
Total forest land	263,992

Data source: Ministry of Environment of Indonesia (1998)

Table 3.2 Land status and burnt area

Land status	Total area burnt (ha)
Non-forest land cleared by burning	16,186
Burnt by escaped fires	8,444
Plantations	88,237
Other	4,391
Total non-forest land	117,258

Data source: Ministry of Environment of Indonesia (1998)

Table 3.3 Fire-related damage in US$ millions

Type of Loss	Loss to Indonesia	Loss to other countries	Total
Timber	493.7	–	493.7
Agriculture	470.4	–	470.4
Direct forest benefits	705.0	–	705.0
Indirect forest benefits	1,077.1	–	1,077.1
Capturable biodiversity	30.0	–	30.0
Firefighting costs	11.7	13.4	25.1
Carbon release	–	272.1	272.1
Total loss due to fire	2,787.9	285.5	3,073.4

Data source: Economy and Environment Program for Southeast Asia and World Wildlife Fund (1998)

Table 3.4 Haze-related damage in US$ millions

Type of loss	Loss to Indonesia	Loss to other countries	Total
Short-term health	924.0	16.8	940.8
Tourism	70.4	185.8	256.2
Other	17.6	181.5	199.1
Total loss due to haze	1,012.0	384.1	1,396.1

Data source: Economy and Environment Program for Southeast Asia and World Wildlife Fund (1998) referents. However, by contrast, the AFC was of sudden onset and wider in scope of impact.

The haze of 1997 affected many Southeast Asian countries and triggered the Regional Haze Action Plan (RHAP). This was immediately adopted and led to the launch of the annual ASEAN Ministerial Meeting on Haze. The RHAP was introduced to strengthen regional capabilities and support the national efforts. The EU member states were supportive of ASEAN's regional integrative efforts. France and Germany were among the international donors to support the RHAP's implementation. Their contribution was part of a bulk amount given to Indonesia by international donors. While this issue has been of concern to Southeast Asia as a whole and has attracted European attention, the ASEAN–EU relationship did not systematically address this issue and support ASEAN regional efforts.

The RHAP was not ASEAN's first attempt at regional cooperation on pollution. In 1990, at the 4th ASEAN Ministerial Meeting on the Environment in Kuala Lumpur, transboundary pollution had been on the agenda and resulted in the Accord on the Environment and Development. In 1992, ASEAN's environmental ministers agreed to harmonise policy directions, starting with cooperation on transboundary air pollution that made reference to the haze. The problem of the haze was addressed in the major ASEAN environmental documents throughout the 1990s.

In 1995, the ASEAN Meeting on the Management of Transboundary Pollution adopted the ASEAN Cooperation Plan on Transboundary Pollution. This agreement was vague and unbinding but managed to formulate a regional approach that was complemented by national measures. In 1995, the Haze Technical Task Force was created, but remained ineffective in its response to the 1997 haze. ASEAN member states preferred national initiatives. In 1999, the Haze Technical Task Force approved the Operational RHAP (ORHAP) that laid out the framework for ASEAN states to pursue activities of prevention, mitigation and monitoring (Nguitragool 2010: 67). The following years saw the implementation of ORHAP.

On 25 November 2003, the Haze Agreement or ASEAN Agreement on Transboundary Haze came into force. This document provided the binding legal framework for the RHAP. However, as of 2012, this document is still not ratified by all ASEAN member states. Indonesia does not want any form of external interference on the haze issue. A binding commitment on the regional level is a sensitive matter. Instead, Indonesia initiated the Sub-Regional Ministerial Steering Committee on Transboundary Haze Pollution. This Committee is shaped by Indonesia's national counter-haze strategy. Despite this setback for regional integration in managing the haze, ASEAN has continued to make attempts to advance on this issue, as manifest in the annual Conference of the Parties to the Haze Agreement, the establishment of the Haze Fund and the various regional and bilateral simulation exercises. The haze has become an issue area in its own right within ASEAN's community-building process and is part of the agenda of the ASEAN Socio-Cultural Community.

Over the years, the threat of the haze has not diminished and in 2006 another severe spread was observed (ASEAN environmental ministers 2006). In spite of limitations due to the ASEAN Way, in 1997, various international actors contributed significantly to the management of the fires and smoke. These actors ranged from the European Commission to the World Wildlife Fund and the Asian Development Bank to state agencies of the USA, Singapore and other countries (Dennis 1999: 33–47).

European assistance on the haze issue

European state and non-state actors have observed with interest the regional integrative dynamics to manage the haze. They have been supportive of the regional ambition, however, the process did not offer an opportunity for the Europeans to become involved (interview with GIZ staff, 26 May 2010). Since the EU is remote and its member states hardly suffer from this form of transboundary air pollution, the likelihood of strong issue-convergence is low. While there has been assistance to combat the haze, these efforts appeared sporadic and seemed to depend on the severity of the haze in any given year.

An Indonesian public servant observed in reference to the haze issue that "they [the Europeans] offered a bit of aid, but aid also has some problems, because when they give aid, Indonesia does not get the full aid, they want European experts and so they also spend the money on the European side" (interview with ASEAN member state official, 31 May 2010). Her colleague added that, with regard to NTS concerns in general, "sometimes you can say that [the] European Union does not understand the problem" (interview with ASEAN member state official, 31 May 2010). While there seems to be a certain degree of awareness that there has been European support to Indonesia in managing the haze problem, it seems that the Indonesian side does not fully agree with European approaches to development cooperation, in general. Furthermore, the interviewed officials highlighted that they were "aware mostly of aid by individual member states". Both the member states and the European Commission have provided assistance to tackle the haze, as will be discussed in the following paragraphs.

In the 1980s and early 1990s, European assistance was predominantly member state assistance and revolved around fighting the fires that caused the haze. For instance, in October 1983, the *Gesellschaft für Technische Zusammenarbeit* (GTZ, now *Gesellschaft für Internationale Zusammenarbeit* (GIZ)), funded by the German Government, was involved in researching and providing technical assistance in two projects in East Kalimantan. The support was short-term and practice-oriented and served as a good baseline for future cooperation. From 26 June to 3 July 1992, the European Commission sent a mission to Sumatra for capacity-building and training purposes. This short-term envoy paved the way for long-term European missions that went beyond capacity-building and addressing the underlying causes of the haze. This initial phase of European action was marked by pragmatism and short-termism, and could be considered as a confidence-building phase. These early projects focused on fire control (interview with GIZ staff, 26 May 2010). They showed significant overlap leaving room for improvement in terms of the coordination of assistance.

The second phase emerged in parallel with the EU's heightened politicisation of its development policy in the early 1990s. While the end of the Cold War compelled the EU and its member states to increasingly pursue a comprehensive foreign policy in their external relations, it also sharpened ideological differences. The ideational dimension conditioned the projects addressing the haze in Indonesia in the 1990s. One long-term project was initiated in 1995 as part of the EU's Forestry Programme for Indonesia. The EU Fire Response Group and the Indonesian Ministry of Forestry launched the Forest Fire Prevention and Control Project with an initial budget of US$4,879,759 for a seven-year period (Dennis 1998). The Forest Fire Prevention and Control Project linked EU activities with the local community level in South Sumatra.

The objective of the Forest Fire Prevention and Control Project was to provide both short-term remedies (e.g. give information and advice on alternative land-clearing techniques, along with warning letters from the government on punitive action, and organise public awareness campaigns) and long-term ones (create job opportunities and raise the economic standard in rural areas) (Dennis 1998). Initially, the Forest Fire Prevention and Control Project was designed as a pre-emptive firefighting and capacity-building project. The severe haze developments in 1997 expanded the scope of this project to include immediate crisis responses.

This project was supported by state-affiliated development agencies and EU member state agencies, including the Department for International Development (DFID). These state and state-affiliated agencies were important in the implementation of the initiatives. They were involved in the training of firefighters, satellite monitoring, early warning, fire danger rating and other activities with the Indonesian side. Sharing European knowledge presents an opportunity for Southeast Asia to acquire new technologies and practices. At the same time, European norms and standards are transferred. The long-term dimension of this project focused on improving the structural conditions surrounding issues of impunity, transparency and best practices.

This initiative was followed by the European Commission's South Sumatra Forest Fire Management Project, which was operational from 2003 to 2008. Over these years, haze-related assistance by the European Commission evolved from practical short-term assistance to comprehensive long-term support. The EU's support linked between the sectors and included multiple stakeholders from the rural population to the ministerial officials and the business elite. Over time, these projects have increasingly targeted the various underlying facets of the haze problem. A GIZ official looking back on the anti-haze projects commented that "it was, if I am not mistaken, very successful and we developed generic guidelines or procedures, so they have well-documented lessons learnt and we even had to distribute some of the lessons learnt in a best-practice-manual, distributed on the regional as well as national level" (interview with GIZ staff, 26 May 2010). The activities aimed at strengthening participatory elements and sustainable development.

The GIZ rated its engagement under this scheme as a success in terms of raising local and national awareness, capacity-building, enhancing coordination and information exchange among the ministries (interview with GIZ staff, 26 May 2010). Early European projects, such as the GIZ project in October 1983, were concerned with direct firefighting responses. The more recent projects were designed to improve the living standards of the rural population and offer alternative sources of income to the various stakeholders involved in land-burning practices (interview with GIZ staff, 25 May 2010). European non-state implementing agencies have been important actors on behalf of the European Commission and member states in implementing the various EU-member-state-funded initiatives.

After the end of the Cold War, the European Commission's competences in the EU's external affairs expanded significantly and the European Commission has become a prominent assistance provider to tackle environmental issues in Asia; it has been integral in commissioning anti-haze projects. These anti-haze initiatives involved multiple stakeholders, ranging from ministerial counterparts to non-governmental actors on the grass-roots level. In 1997, the European Commission enhanced cooperation with the Indonesian Ministry of Forestry and sought to incorporate both long-term and short-term elements within the anti-haze response (Dennis 1999). The EU Fire Response Group monitored, assessed and collated information on the fires in Sumatra and Kalimantan. The Group further determined the liaison and coordination with other international donors. The Monitoring Tropical Vegetation Unit of the Joint Research Centre of the European Commission launched two research activities to detect, map and determine the deforestation and biomass loss of the burnt areas. Additionally, Denmark, Finland, France, Sweden and the United Kingdom channelled considerable sums through the UN institutions to assist Indonesia in managing the negative effects of the fires and haze in 1997 (Dennis 1999: 54–59).

Today, the environmental agenda has altered and the haze is no longer an immediate objective of the European Commission's and the EU member states' engagement in Southeast Asia. A GIZ official explains "[t]wo years ago, the two most important topics were the Forest Law Enforcement, Governance and Trade (FLEGT) and Reducing Emissions from Deforestation and Forest Degradation, before that, haze has been an important issue, of course, it is still linked to some of those issues" (interview with GIZ staff, 26 May 2010). Currently, the European Commission, the EU member states and the implementing agencies are more concerned with addressing the underlying causes, common to an array of environmental issues. *De facto*, the haze issue lacked and still lacks salience within the ASEAN–EU relationship. It does not act as a stimulus for lasting inter-regional cooperation.

The severe crisis in 1997 worsened the impact of the AFC on the livelihoods of the Indonesian people and strengthened the negative perceptions towards the Indonesian authorities. One could argue that the haze was one of the factors leading to the toppling of the Indonesian regime. In the years that followed, the end of the Suharto era has hardened Indonesia's proclivity to national sovereignty and the treatment of the haze was considered a domestic issue that should not involve ASEAN member states.

If ASEAN manages to overcome the deadlock on the regional level, the EU would very likely be interested reigniting its support to ASEAN in making resources available to find solutions to the haze (interview with GIZ staff, 26 May 2010). A GIZ official said that the haze "used to be discussed, but there are many limitations and political problems involved, if ASEAN were to identify this as a priority area, we will of course indicate our support" (interview with GIZ staff, 26 May 2010).

In summary, European activities prior, during and in the aftermath of the haze crisis of 1997 can be summed up as technical assistance. They were both pre-emptive and responsive, and an important part of the international assistance to support Indonesia's quest for fire prevention and control (Dennis 1999). Currently, European environmental and agricultural engagement focuses on combating the underlying social causes that trigger the haze problem.

Overall, the success of the international assistance has been mixed. In the absence of a more affordable method of land-clearing that is accessible to all layers of society, the forest fires are likely to continue. Fire is the cheapest way of clearing land and is a custom of land-clearing among rural farmers. Sharing and enhancing support in research to develop alternative land-clearing methods for farmers is vital and needed.

This chapter has shown that in spite of the localised nature of the haze issue, the European Commission and the EU member states have been interested in providing assistance and becoming involved.[1] This suggests that the EU's motivation to assist is not conditioned solely by converging threat perceptions. It further indicates the pertinence of the developmental perspective in understanding the EU's engagement.

The role of non-state European actors

The GIZ and other agencies have been integral European actors when implementing the anti-haze activities. They act in accordance with the ministerial guidelines of their countries and, at the same time, they seek to uphold the EU's core values and norms, while attempting to maximise effectiveness. A GIZ official explained,

> Very specifically we have a comparative advantage to some other donors, also, to the official and high-level European engagement in the region, and that at least at the technical level, we do have quite some flexibility also to get officials, also lower level officials of Myanmar involved in our programme.
>
> (interview with GIZ staff, 26 May 2010)

State-affiliated and non-state implementing actors are more flexible on political issues in the ASEAN–EU relationship and can avoid the normative commitments of the official level. In Chapter 1, the discussion of the engagement of such actors with Myanmar highlighted the extent to which these actors ensured cooperation without putting their governments in a sticky position in regard to their political and normative agenda. Non-state actors as implementers have greater understanding of the local realities. They can better design projects that do not defy local sensitivities and meet the normative objectives of the contractor. Southeast Asian officials indicated that these European non-state actors play an exceptional role during the implementation process of development projects (interview with ASEAN ISIS representative, 31 October 2008). Thus, understanding the EU as an actor requires us to pay close attention to these non-state actors.

The European Commission and its member states are bound to their official rhetoric and normative agenda. At the same time, the people-dimension is a very important objective of the EU's external engagement and an essential aspect of the EU's identity. The normative agenda confines the EU's and its member states' scope of engagement and, thus, they may fall short in alleviating the plight of persons affected by NTS crises. Some instruments employed by the EU and its member states may not necessarily promote the people-dimension within some partner countries. In principle, the EU avoids official dialogue with regimes that systematically abuse human rights and violate various norms and values of the EU. In these instances, the EU and its member states sometimes resort to unofficial channels of communication through non-state actors who act as proxies.[2]

Generally speaking, the more these non-state actors are funded by the European people directly, the higher is the consistency with the EU's normative identity, since they do not have to follow through policy guidelines. Implementing state-affiliated agencies take action according to international normative standards and their conception of situative 'good' development cooperation, but remain in line with the guiding principles and objectives provided by the ministries (interview with GIZ staff, 25 May 2010). As a dependent contractor they are committed to the effectiveness of the assignment and pleasing the contracting entity.

In contrast to state-affiliated actors, non-state actors that are funded and steered by civil society are more flexible when implementing their own agenda. They can translate their normative convictions into action seemingly one-to-one. When the haze of 1997 spread, Greenpeace's Southeast Asia climate and energy campaigner Athena Ronquillo-Ballesteros complained about the ASEAN member states' inability to manage the haze. Although it is the local Greenpeace showing activism, we need to conceive the actions as part of a larger global movement, since Greenpeace Indonesia is also supported by European counterparts and donors.

Non-state actors on site are flexible and possess local expertise and, therefore, they are important when European donors require effective implementation that may not be in line with their official normative rhetoric. Technocratisation is implicit to some niche areas of cooperation and can occur in some instances of NTS threat convergence. Non-state actors may well be part of this process. However, non-state actors lessen the extent of state-steered technocratisation within countries by absorbing the burden of implementation and administration. Issue-specific cooperation and management of NTS threats stimulate integration across states and provide an opportunity for the non-state level to establish itself as an alternative, community-oriented and grassroots bottom-up level.

For example, in the case of the haze in 1983, the GIZ, as a significant non-state actor on anti-haze efforts in Southeast Asia, was funded by the German Government to research and provide technical assistance to two projects in East Kalimantan. Furthermore, the GIZ conducted a study on the health impacts of the haze in the 1990s and implemented the Integrated Forest Fire Management Project in East Kalimantan. The second phase of this project ended in 2000. Another German non-state actor involved in tackling the haze was the Hanns Seidel Foundation. This political foundation directly supported the project on Strengthening ASEAN's Capacity to Prevent and Mitigate Transboundary Atmospheric Pollution Resulting from Forest Fires (RETA 5778-REG) with funds and interns. The University of Freiburg in Germany established a Southeast Asia Fire Monitoring Centre to link up with the activities of ORHAP (ASEAN and Asian Development Bank researchers 2001: 220–221). The activities of these non-state actors are primarily technical and are not necessarily a case of explicit norms and values promotion of the EU.

While European non-state actors are important implementing actors for the EU, they are also dependent on the liaising capacities and resources of the European Commission and the EU member states. Before development cooperation proceeds, the EU and its member states are actively engaging Southeast Asian governments to agree on the advancement of certain projects. Often, European actors have found it difficult to persuade Southeast Asian states to adopt many of the devised projects in entirety. Authorities within Southeast Asian countries are wary of extensive external influence and tend to value economic growth over environmental protection. At present, when it comes to environmental protection, it is mainly the ASEAN Secretariat and the democratising ASEAN states, including Indonesia, which are willing to be persuaded by Western ideas of regionalism. The Indonesian government post-Suharto had difficulties regulating the forestry sector. This power vacuum, combined with the will of soft reformers within the government to restructure the forestry sector, provided a favourable local environment for the EU to initiate projects to improve forest governance. During Suharto's period in power, such proposals faced constant rejection and lacked implementation. While Indonesia is still sceptical of external interference, it sees the economic and political benefits from its openness (interview with EU official, 27 May 2010).

Central characteristics of the EU as an actor

It is important for the EU to assist Southeast Asia in a comprehensive manner, because structural changes on the domestic level are paramount when it comes to the success or failure of the projects. The EU has understood that sector-specific objectives are intertwined with the normative and material setting. Newly designed European projects to address NTS threats in Southeast Asia attempt to incorporate multiple stakeholders into the decision-making process, be more people-oriented and emphasise the role of non-state actors. They aim to diffuse the power monopoly of the state and the military in the partner country, increase the transparency and strengthen the role of regional authorities.

Similarly to the first case of the AFC, the case of the haze is associated with fields of governance, namely, agriculture and forestry that are traditionally located in the realm of socio-economic politics. However, in the last two decades, these realms of the low politics have increasingly experienced processes of securitisation. Specifically, in regard to the environmental sector, the EU and its member states have been at the forefront of securitisation. The EU and other international actors have been convincing developing countries of the nexus between environmental issues and their people's plight. They have managed to push the topic, with particular reference to climate change, onto the global agenda of security concerns (High Representative and European Commission 2008). The EU's ambition in securitising the environmental field echoes the NTS concerns of many developing countries. On the one hand, it gives insights into the EU's normative inclinations. On the other, this emphasises the EU's economic and power calculations as an advanced economic power that is not a hegemon in the Asia-Pacific.

The EU and Southeast Asia share the perception that the environment is an important common good to be protected, but the strategies and perceptions differ. There are socio-economic, geographic and climatic cleavages that fuel the different degrees of affectedness. This constrains the EU as an actor from the outset. The difference in climatic and socio-economic factors is a problem for the relationship between the two regions, as well as within the two regions. Intra-regional perceptions on environmental issues diverge and complicate a coherent external position. Against this backdrop of internal incoherence, it becomes difficult for the EU to persuade and convince other regions about the benefits of its environmental norms. In fact, Southeast Asian officials have pointed to the internal cleavages within the EU and have argued that the environmental sector is not only a problem between the ASEAN and EU side, but also within the EU itself (interview with ASEAN member state official, 31 May 2010). If the ASEAN–EU level does not agree on political output in this field, the ASEAN side cannot be blamed (interview with ASEAN member state official, 31 May 2010).

Given the various supranational, state and non-state anti-haze activities, one can question whether the EU can be considered as a collective actor as such. This chapter revealed that the EU as an actor consisted of many heads. Juxtaposing the EU as an actor to other international actors suggests that European activities rank similarly in scope and impact (Dennis 1999: 14–15). Generally, European activities were responsive and peaked in times of severe events of the haze. The activities addressed both the long- and short-term dimensions and aimed at sustainable community development. They demonstrated that the EU evolved from a short-term and practice-oriented actor to an actor with long-term ambitions.

In the early phase of engagement, European activities were short-term, technical and relied on confidence-building measures. They were responsive and appeared demand-oriented, focused on providing a quick relief to the problem. They aimed at firefighting, both literally and figuratively. Over the years, the activities revealed a shift in focus increasingly addressing the underlying issues. In the 1990s, this evolution paralleled the European Commission's expansion of its competency in foreign affairs. The European Commission's outward orientation increased and placed emphasis on a comprehensive external approach.

The second phase of engagement to tackle the haze focused on long-term projects that did not combat the fires and the haze directly. During this phase, the EU increasingly addressed the underlying causes of the haze problem. These long-term projects from the mid-1990s onwards suggest that the EU has become more interested in projecting and diffusing its standards. Aware of globalisation and interdependence, the EU has recognised that it needs to shape the global level according to its standards to safeguard itself and keep other regions stable.

The haze is a threat to the welfare of states and people in Southeast Asia, but the EU's comprehensive developmental approach to address this threat is not defined as a security measure. From a European perspective, the EU and its member states did not regard their engagement along the lines of security and did not actively securitise the haze to increase development assistance to Indonesia. In fact, the severity of the haze events replaced the necessity of securitisation. The EU views its external assistance as development aid to defuse the recurrence of the land and forest fires. Both the authorities and people within the provinces that the EU anti-haze initiatives targeted perceived the EU's forest fire-related activities as an act of development assistance and less as an act of human survival (interview with GIZ staff, 25 May 2010).

The divergence in socio-economic development and conceptions of security underline the ambiguities of an NTS perspective. While the utility of the NTS frame in this case study is questionable, it is nevertheless analytically useful in many other cases of environmental problems in Southeast Asia that have impacted on the security of the state (McNeil 2002).

Conclusions

This chapter has displayed the EU as a short- and long-term-oriented actor, whose engagement was both responsive and pre-emptive. Through long-term initiatives that targeted the underlying causes of the haze and through considerable involvement of implementing state-affiliated agencies and non-state actors, it was argued that the EU attempted to project and uphold its norms and values. In relation to this, the concept of an actor by proxy was introduced, raising the necessity for academics to incorporate non-state or state-affiliated actors into scholarly definitions of the EU as an actor in Southeast Asia.

Similarly to the previous case of the AFC, the nature of the crisis is a factor in determining the foreign policy method of the EU. The projects were generally between European actors and Indonesia, and lacked an inter-regional dimension. The European Commission and the EU member states perceive the haze mainly as a localised and Indonesian problem. While EU interest is important to initiate assistance, it is also imperative to take into account domestic dynamics and normative foundations within the ASEAN region. It was suggested that if ASEAN's regional integration process to manage the haze should advance, there may be opportunities for the EU to step in.

Notes

1 The EU has also engaged in discussions with Southeast Asia on transboundary pollution and forest protection within a variety of dialogue fora. From the 1980s, forest matters were discussed within the ASEAN–EC JCC and since the 1990s, environmental issues have been part of the ASEAN–EU ministerial agenda. In 1986, within the JCC framework, the ASEAN Timber Technology Centre was founded in Malaysia. Although the initial JCC cooperation appeared to be limited to economic interests, it was visible that the high environmental standards of the European side compelled the transfer of norms and structural adaption. Although the EU may pursue economic interests, its interaction with less-developed actors forces these to adapt. The adaptation on the side of its counterpart

to meet European expectations for trade purposes shows that the EU has an influence in sectors that may be vulnerable to NTS threats.
2 The actor by proxy concept was inspired by comments from Prof. Jürgen Rüland at the Collaborative Colloquium at the Southeast Asian Studies section of the Albert-Ludwigs University in Freiburg on 11 February 2011.

4 EU assistance in light of the Bali Bombings and avian influenza

The two previous chapters have referred to the EU as an actor in cases that took place in 1997, in a time when Southeast Asia was experiencing an upheaval of its normative foundations. The Southeast Asian side considered these crises as security concerns for both the state and the people. These crises stimulated a paradigmatic shift in the way regional integration was conceptualised and necessitated opening towards new norms and practices. They also triggered increased European awareness and engagement in Southeast Asia to assist in socio-economic development. However, it was not until the September 11 attacks that the EU and its member states adopted a stronger security perspective towards the region. The bombings in Kuta on the island of Bali on 12 October 2002 further sharpened the EU's security perspective on the region. The bombings took the lives of 202 people and injured 209 (Australian Federal Police 2008). European countries that had citizens injured or killed immediately offered assistance and stayed in close contact with the Indonesian authorities that were attempting to advance investigations, while coping with the considerable revenue loss, in particular within the tourism industry.

This act of terrorism, linked to the al-Qaeda[1]-affiliated Jemaah Islamiah (JI), was a major shock to Indonesia. The attacks tested Indonesian policy-makers and stimulated greater Indonesian counter-terrorist cooperation with external powers. Specifically, the cooperative efforts with the major security partners the USA and Australia intensified after the bombings. The attacks also stimulated greater regional integrative dynamics. A Southeast Asian think tank representative suggested that, since the bombings, officials as well as ASEAN ISIS and other Track 2 institutions have actively discussed terrorism in Southeast Asia (Interview with ASEAN ISIS representative 31 October 2008). While the attacks triggered greater intra-regional communication on the Track 2 level, counter-terrorism remained a policy area that was jealously guarded by states and dependent on bilateral cooperation with external partners. The following section illustrates the cooperation with the EU

The terrorist threat from the ASEAN–EU perspective

Within the ASEAN–EU context, insurgencies and international terrorism have been problems that the Southeast Asian and EU states have been facing over many decades. The terrorist concern was placed on the ASEAN–EU inter-regional agenda at the 6th ASEAN–EC Ministerial Meeting in Jakarta on 20–21 October 1986. A terrorist attack by Libyan terrorists on a West Berlin discotheque popular among Americans in April of 1986 led to an incorporation of international terrorism into the dialogue and an exchange of views on this between the two regions.[2] Both sides covenanted to cooperate closely and agreed on the necessity of sharing experiences and embracing a comprehensive approach beyond the narrow strategic-military thinking.

In 1988, the EC and ASEAN member states declared that they will seek to find "political solutions to the problems which form the roots of terrorism" (ASEAN and EC member states 1988: para. 27). In the 1990s, the topic vanished from the agenda and was overshadowed by the new international structure and the various new issues on the agenda that ranged from environmental concerns to disarmament and arms control. International terrorism reappeared on the agenda in 1997 as one of many points discussed within the newly modified political and security ASEAN–EU dialogue, following the comprehensive strategy outlined at the 12th AEMM in Karlsruhe.

By then, the ARF and ASEM had been established to create alternative fora to discuss this issue. Since international terrorism was not perceived as a major threat to the EU and ASEAN member states, this lurking menace was not closely examined within the three fora until 2001. It was not until the September 11 attacks that the threat of international terrorism was brought to the top of the regional and inter-regional political agenda.

At ASEM 4 on 22–24 September 2002, international terrorism overshadowed the summit. This was prior to the Bali Bombings and showed that the September 11 attacks heightened the threat perceptions of both the ASEAN and EU member states. However, there was still some distance and scepticism towards the American approach. In Southeast Asia, some governments were wary about the American influence, while others embraced this as an opportunity to coalesce with the Americans and tackle domestic insurgencies. Despite a sense of solidarity towards the USA, which was formalised in the signing of the US–ASEAN Joint Declaration for Cooperation to Combat International Terrorism on 1 August 2002 and the US–EU Terrorism Pact on 25 June 2003, it was the terrorist attacks within the respective regions that ultimately galvanised national efforts. The member states that were at the centre stage of the attacks were under pressure to improve and develop their existing counter-terrorist measures.

In particular, in the aftermath of the Madrid and London attacks, Spain and the UK played leading roles in promoting resilience on the EU regional level. Al-Qaeda in Europe claimed responsibility for the bombings and showed Europe in a painful manner that the EU, too, was the target of violent acts by international terrorism. The ten bombs detonated on four commuter trains in Madrid on 11 March 2004, killed 191 people and injured up to 1800 people (*The Guardian*, 2007). This bombing was the moment-generating attack for Spain. These attacks suggested that the new measures introduced in the aftermath of the attacks on the Twin Towers were either lagging behind in implementation or did not suffice. This compelled the EU member states to revisit and enhance their efforts.

Already in 2003, the ESS identified that "Europe is both a target and a base for terrorism: European countries are targets and have been attacked. Logistical bases for al-Qaeda cells have been uncovered in the UK, Italy, Germany, Spain and Belgium" (Council of the European Union 2003: 3). International terrorism as an external threat had gained local reach and more action was required. The attacks raised concerns about the degree of preparedness of the EU and its member states, and the public seemed to be sceptical towards the illiberal nature of some of the new anti-terrorist measures.

Although domestic terrorist attacks have the primer action-generating effect, severe acts of terrorism overseas contributed to Europe's increased awareness of international terrorism post-September 11. The Bali Bombings were not a threat to Europe. They neither triggered any united European conception of Southeast Asia as a source of the terrorist threat nor directly led to domestic policy impulses within the EU. However, in light of the continuously operating al-Qaeda training camps in Southeast Asia (Gunaratna 2006: 4), there are some EU member states that have adopted a securitised understanding of Southeast Asia in relation to the issue of international terrorism.

The threat posed by al-Qaeda in Europe is of a different nature. In Southeast Asia, the threat revolves around local terrorism that may or may not receive support from international terrorist organisations for its operations. The EU member states "agree to disagree" on the linkage between local and international terrorism in Southeast Asia (interview with EU member state official, 24 May 2010). Within the EU, it is al-Qaeda itself that is the synonym for the terrorist threat. Old terrorism has faded away (Neumann 2009). The terrorist threat of today emanates particularly from the internationally networked al-Qaeda cells and the local jihadist groups which "are coalescing into a united front prepared to follow Osama bin Laden's global strategy" (Brooke and Leiken 2005). Domestic nationalist and ideological terrorist groups are widely considered as a phenomenon of the past. By contrast, in Southeast Asia, old terrorism persists and risks entangling itself in al-Qaeda's international network.

The Western world is still the desirable target for al-Qaeda. However, "[w]ith the difficulty of striking targets in North America, Europe, Australia and New Zealand, al-Qaeda and its associated groups are aggressively scouting for targets in lawless zones of Asia, Africa, and the Middle East" (Gunaratna 2006: 5). Aurel Croissant observed that since 2001, the Thailand–Philippines–Indonesia area is part of the five major areas in the world where over 80 per cent of the terrorist incidents occur (Croissant and Schwank 2006: 12). Southeast Asia functions as a logistical and launching base for terrorist acts by al-Qaeda, as exemplified through the operations leading to the September 11 attacks (Gunaratna 2002: 232–270). In light of this reality and the fact that terrorism is not a new phenomenon, it is imperative for the EU and its member states to step up interest in managing the extremist and terrorist threat in Southeast Asia and enhancing activities within this region, although terrorism is perceived differently among Southeast Asian countries.

Specifically, in the aftermath of the Bali Bombings, the EU and the member states were quick to condemn the attacks[3] and declared solidarity with Indonesia. In the Council's conclusions, the Council supported the European Commission's "intention to consider Indonesia as a pilot country for assistance in the implementation of [UN Security Council Resolution (UNSCR)] 1373" and further "[a]ccelerate EU assistance to Indonesia as well as other parts of South East Asia in other fields relevant to the fight against terrorism, including good governance, rule of law and border monitoring" (European Council 2002).

Within the ASEAN–EU dialogue, at the 14th ASEAN–EU Ministerial Meeting of 27–28 January 2003 a joint effort to combat terrorism was initiated by both sides. The Joint Declaration on Cooperation to Combat Terrorism was adopted in line with the UN provisions. It said,

> As a follow to the Declaration, an ASEAN–EU Consultation was held in Ha Noi in June 2003. During the Consultation, both ASEAN and the EU stressed the desire for a regional approach and agreed to focus their cooperative efforts particularly in the following areas: technical

assistance and capacity building in regional counter-terrorism operations and systems; border security, including travel document security and combating trafficking in persons particularly in women and children; immigration border control including customs procedures; cooperation among law enforcement agencies; programmes/projects on anti-money laundering and suppression of terrorist financing; new techniques/technologies to combat money laundering; adoption of international anti-money laundering standards and exchange of best practices; development of Financial Intelligence Units (FIUs), exchange of experts and bank regulators; funding for computer equipment and software for FIUs; and training for bankers specifically in reporting of suspicious transactions.

(Pushpanathan 2003)

At the meeting, a variety of areas of potential collaboration were envisaged. Following the Ha Noi Consultation, the European Commission agreed to undertake an RRM assessment mission to the region and explore these suggestions. Based on the agreed Terms of Reference, ASEAN members and the EU aimed to organise the mission jointly. The launch of the RRM was not without controversy. The European Commission did not consider conditioning assistance and linking the RRM to Indonesia's human rights record. For the purpose of offering immediate support, Indonesia's human rights track record was overlooked. Given the urgency that crises exude, an actor has to balance between timeliness of action and identity conflicts. The EU declared in its ASEAN Regional Indicative Programme 2005–2006,

It will endeavour to build a regional capacity to assist ASEAN members to implement UNSCR 1373, and to address the impact of terrorist activities. As a first step the [European Commission] has deployed an expert mission to investigate possible areas for this cooperation. In assessing its support the [European Commission] looked at measures which could have an added value at regional level and which could be coherent with the [Commission] Country Strategy and ongoing projects in this field. It was decided at the ASEAN-EU Senior Officials Meeting on transnational crime in Hanoi (June 2003) that the mission should focus on two fairly broad issues: a) border management and immigration control and b) anti-money laundering/combating terrorist financing....The subsequent expert mission to the ASEAN region found that border management offered better prospects of successful (first time) cooperation between the EU and ASEAN than fight against 'financing of terrorism'. 'Financing of terrorism' requires much more country-specific actions, notably on the law enforcement side.

(European Commission 2004: para. 5.3.1)

The two paragraphs illustrate how initial ambitions touching upon various possible areas of common action were narrowed down to two areas of potential European engagement. The European Commission concentrated on the improvement of existing national border management systems and capacities of regional border management cooperation to achieve an Integrated Border Management System. Awareness training and document security were provided over an implementation period of three years starting from 2006. The budget for this endeavour accounted for €4–6 million for 2005–2006. By the time the implementation phase started, the ASEAN side seemed to have lost interest and the regional approach was aborted (interview with EU official, 27 May 2010). Alternatively, bilateral projects were pursued; and with the Philippines a border management initiative was implemented through inter-agential cooperation between 2006 and 2009.

Specifically, as a response to the Bali Bombings in the area of anti-money laundering, the European Commission "initiated support in the area of counter-terrorism, through backing anti-money laundering activities and assistance to the Jakarta Centre of Law Enforcement Co-operation (JCLEC) under the Rapid Reaction Mechanism" (European Commission 2002: 5.2). The EU displayed the expertise and goodwill to assist Southeast Asia. However, the EU's ambitions fell short of implementation. The initiative on anti-money laundering under RRM lacked the necessary appeal to Southeast Asia. In fact, an EU official argued that the decisions on the projects are not only based on what the counterpart needs, but are also a matter of how you approach and attract the interest of the Southeast Asian counterpart (interview with EU official, 27 May 2010). Understanding of domestic realities and sensitivities goes hand in hand with official commitments.

For example, the EU committed to support so-called counter-terrorist or law enforcement centres in Southeast Asia (ASEAN and EU member states 2005: para. 7). The European Commission's contribution to these centres ranked below that of the individual member states and the share of other external powers. *De facto*, there has not been any financial contribution by the EU and its member states to International Law Enforcement Academy (ILEA) since the adoption of the Joint Declaration in 2003. ILEA was founded in 1999 and has since then been jointly funded by the USA and Thailand. The USA has been allocating more than 90 per cent of the Centre's budget. Since its establishment there have been only two courses that were sponsored by the Europeans: one in 2007 and one in 2008. The Southeast Asia Regional Centre for Counter Terrorism (SEARCCT) was created on 1 July 2003 and, since then, only France and the UK have provided some courses.

The law enforcement centre in Jakarta seems to attract more European assistance both from member states and the European Commission. In contrast to the courses offered at ILEA, the courses at JCLEC address counter-terrorism directly. The British Embassy has sponsored projects and is on JCLEC's board of supervisors. Since JCLEC became operational in 2004, the British have hosted various counter-terrorist workshops and courses there. In general, the UK has been the most active European country in Indonesia on counter-terrorism cooperation, and also elsewhere in Southeast Asia. The Danish have also funded courses on Advanced Analysis of Terrorist Organisations and Operations and one on Islamic Law and Politics in 2006. Spain funded the Counter Terrorism Investigations Management course from 14 January to 1 February 2008.

The main motivation behind European counter-terrorism activism in Southeast Asia seems to stem from the historical ties of former European colonial powers and former Southeast Asian colonies. In the case of the UK, this engagement has been facilitated by various existing defence and intelligence ties, in particular, the Five Eyes Alliance and the Five Power Defence Arrangements. Furthermore, the Netherlands, the UK and France have shown significant interest in counter-terrorism, because their citizens have also been the main European tourists affected by the bombings in Bali. While international ties and events with shock impact are key drivers behind European interest in extra-regional counter-terrorism activities, national threat and urgency perceptions of new terrorism are also essential motivations behind European actions.

The latter explains the engagement of the Danish in Southeast Asia. As a small European country with a limited foreign and security policy apparatus, it is surprising that Denmark funded a course at JCLEC in 2006. The Mohammed cartoon controversy of September 2005 sparked a widely felt anti-Danish resentment within the Muslim world. In the years after the cartoon controversy, various anti-Danish protests took place and attacks on Danish embassies occurred. Denmark became caught up in the War on Terror campaign. A Danish state official described the cartoon controversy as a second decisive moment after September 11, which changed Denmark's terrorist alert (interview with EU member state official, 24 May 2010). Since then, Southeast Asia has become more important to Denmark from a security perspective and security advisor positions to the Danish embassies have been created throughout the world, including Southeast Asia. The Danish government was compelled to link domestic and international concerns of international terrorism. The dividing line between the internal and external dimensions of counter-terrorism has vanished and the threat narrative for national security has become increasingly contingent on security developments abroad.

To Denmark, terrorism in Southeast Asia is not a localised threat. It is an international threat that requires cooperation with the major regional players in the Asia-Pacific. Being a small state that lacks capacities and resources, Danish engagement in the region is limited to core funding and collaboration with the "bigger players" (interview with EU member state official, 24 May 2010). The American Second Front campaign in Southeast Asia saw the Americans emphasise their own operational role and de-emphasise that of their allies. Danish diplomats said that their country contributed to the American Second Front campaign and was appreciated, however, Denmark "did not see its interests fully realised" (interview with EU member state official, 24 May 2010). Australia and the USA are external actors that dictate the agenda and operationalisation of counter-terrorist activities in the Southeast Asian region (interview with the director of ILEA, 3 December 2009).

The director of ILEA added that there are Europeans, namely the British who have their own facilities in Southeast Asia and offer training. In his years in office, he has only been approached once by an "EU guy" to discuss an ASEAN–EU training course (interview with the director of ILEA, 3 December 2009). Only a few EU member states have taken an interest in collaboration with American partners on counter-terrorism in the region. At the same time, European engagement in this field is sought after by Southeast Asian authorities mainly for funding purposes on a sporadic case-by-case basis. The Bali Bombings were a localised crisis and were not conducive to the EU offering substantial inter-regional best-practice-sharing.

In this context, it is also important to remember that counter-terrorism falls under the competence of the EU member states. It is the member states that hold the prerogative of direct engagement with ASEAN member states. Therefore, the European Commission has to be very careful in packaging EU funding for counter-terrorism purposes. The variation in competences limits the scope of inter-regional experience-sharing *per se*. In keeping with the varying competences, EU collective engagement was limited to actions targeting underlying issues of the terrorist problem.

The European Commission has been an important driving force behind the inter-regional projects within the ASEM framework and the ASEAN–EU dialogue. The ASEAN–EU dialogue echoes the guidelines of the international level and has rested on rhetorical commitments. It is lagging behind the official rhetoric and driven by bilateral ties. Whereas the ASEAN–EU Ministerial Meetings have brought about only one significant counter-terrorist activity between the two regions – the ASEAN–EU Migration and Border Management programme; the ASEM dialogue witnessed greater EU collective agency.

Since the 1st ASEM, combating international terrorism has been part of the inter-regional agenda. However, it was not until the 4th ASEM of 22–23 September 2002 in Copenhagen that ASEM initiated concrete counter-terrorist measures, including the annual Seminar on Anti-Terrorism, now known as the Conference on Counter Terrorism. At Copenhagen, the EU urged the ASEAN member states in 2002 to "develop further their cooperation in this area and emphasised the need to implement the series of activities agreed in the ASEM Copenhagen Co-operation Programme on Fighting International Terrorism of September 2002" (European Council 2002). The EU underlined the commitment to ASEM activities and highlighted the importance of this framework for the ASEAN–EU cooperation on counter-terrorism.

Leaders further adopted the ASEM Copenhagen Declaration on Cooperation against International Terrorism and the ASEM Copenhagen Cooperation Programme on Fighting International Terrorism and for the first time ASEM members convened a session on cultures and civilisations. This session aimed to promote understanding, unity and tolerance among the culturally diverse participants. This cross-cultural concept was to be adopted on all levels of ASEM and promoted by the Asia–Europe Foundation (ASEF), which acts like a secretariat for ASEM.

ASEM emphasises the people-to-people approach in fighting extremism and terrorism, and acknowledged the importance of education in overcoming stereotypes. The ideological and cultural roots of extremism and terrorism are addressed through initiatives like the ASEM Interfaith Dialogue since 2005. These types of initiatives contribute to repealing cultural and religious prejudice. In this context, the EU acts in accordance with its normative identity and actively promotes its norms and values in line with the UN resolutions and with respect for the UN Charter on Human Rights.

ASEM has not produced a unique Asia–Europe perspective on terrorism that was distinct from the American perspective and there are many similarities between the ASEM and American positions on terrorism and the counter-terrorist approach (Robles Jr. 2008: 136–137). Alfredo Robles Jr. further remarked that the importance of international terrorism on the international agenda has also led to a reversal of the founding principles of ASEM, which exclude development assistance and promote an equal partnership. The various ASEM terrorist responses have allowed development assistance to sneak in. At the same time, he criticised that, "[t]here is, however, a risk that these [ASEM] countries and their citizens are increasingly identified with new security threats" and hence, a potential of viewing immigrants from these countries as part of the threat for Europe (Robles Jr. 2008: 138). The developmental perspective was adopted to some extent and appeared to be part of the securitisation developments to enhance ASEAN resilience and safeguard European insecurity from outside challenges.

The EU also supported the counter-terrorism agenda within the ARF. It promoted the expansion of the ARF inter-sessional meetings, conferences, workshops and seminars to address a broad range of terrorist and terrorism-related issues post-September 11. The focus of these ARF initiatives was on best-practice-sharing. In this context, the EU has attempted to share its OSCE experience with ASEAN. Axel Berkofsky observed in 2003 that

> the EU could become more active, using experience gained from OSCE confidence-building and preventive diplomacy mechanisms and strategies to address conflicts in Asia. For instance, France, Germany, Italy and Britain have wide-ranging experience with fighting terrorism, including intelligence gathering and sharing, drafting and implementing anti-terrorist legislation, and trying and convicting suspected terrorists. In all these areas, the EU could assist Asian member states of the ARF individually, as well as the organisation as a whole: perhaps ARF could act as a centre for sharing anti-terrorist intelligence collated by all its member states.
>
> (Berkofsky 2003: 2)

Berkofsky's suggestions are still valid today. However, the opportunities to fully share and transfer the European experience and knowledge are still waiting to be created.

The interviews with ASEAN and EU officials showed a mixed picture of the OSCE's role as a model for the ARF in counter-terrorism. EU officials believe that the OSCE is a good source of inspiration for the ARF, since it strengthens the states from the bottom up. The EU is keen to project the OSCE model, but realises that in the past and even now, it may have been a little bit "pushy" (interview with EU official, 27 May 2010). An official from an EU delegation in Southeast Asia expressed that the current European approach is to sit back and "let the Asian side learn by themselves" (interview with EU official, 27 May 2010). If Southeast Asian governments should approach the EU at some stage in the future, the EU would be ready to assist.

An ASEAN Secretariat official contradicted this and said that the European side seemed keen to showcase the OSCE experience on Preventive Diplomacy to ASEAN. The Europeans offered facilities to show how Preventive Diplomacy is done under the EU framework (interview with ASEAN Secretariat official, 25 May 2010). She did not criticise this European ambition but raised concerns about the general operational manner in which the EU's activities have been conducted (interview with ASEAN Secretariat official, 25 May 2010). They appeared to be indirect, ad hoc and lacking a concrete workplan. In contrast to the American projects, the European projects seemed to lack thorough execution (interview with ASEAN Secretariat official, 25 May 2010). She further argued that the European side strongly supports human rights but appeared more lenient than the USA in many instances (interview with ASEAN Secretariat official, 25 May 2010). Within the ARF, the EU's stance is unclear and "fuzzy" and therefore the Asian side favours the American clear-cut stance and rates the Americans as more accountable and committed to the region (interview with ASEAN Secretariat official, 25 May 2010).

Southeast Asian leaders do not view the EU or even its individual member states as significant security actors in the region. The military support of the American hub-and-spokes system persists as the primary focal point in the field of counter-terrorism. At the same time, it is increasingly supplemented by US technical support and humanitarian assistance; American troops are on site to give combat training and, at the same time, they build schools.

In summary, this sub-chapter revealed that the EU's and its member states' engagement in Southeast Asia appeared to be primarily driven by the perception that societies in Southeast Asia are vulnerable to extremism and require improvement of structural conditions. This perspective varies among EU member states. In fact, domestic threat perceptions and securitisation efforts play an important role, as exemplified through the case of Denmark. On the supranational level, securitisation to assist Southeast Asia was drawn upon to justify financial support. However, the initiatives themselves were framed differently to target the underlying causes of extremism and terrorism.

The case of avian influenza

One year after the Bali Bombings, the Southeast Asian region witnessed another critical NTS challenge. Avian influenza broke out at the end of

2003 among poultry in the region. Many countries attempted to solve the problem by national means and concealed initial outbreaks to avoid public panic. Instead of securitisation, the affected ASEAN states relied on de-securitisation. Many governments were in a state of denial and blamed the poultry deaths on other diseases, including Newcastle disease or fowl cholera. Laos and Thailand initially claimed their outbreaks to be fowl cholera (*The Nation*, 20 January 2004; Agence France Press, 22 January 2004).

Many countries lacked the resources to tackle the outbreaks effectively. It took them weeks to realise and accept this before finally calling for international assistance. Thailand's government had denied the outbreak for weeks and has admitted that it concealed the outbreak to avoid public panic (*International Herald Tribune*, 23 January 2004). Thailand, as the major poultry exporter to the EU and the fourth largest exporter in the world, misinformed EU Health Commissioner David Byrne, who was visiting the avian influenza-affected countries in Southeast Asia to that time. The official statement was that avian influenza did not exist in Thailand. Hence, the EU as the biggest importer of Thai poultry did not place an immediate ban on Thailand's poultry exports (*The Nation*, 20 January 2004). After Byrne's visit, Thailand admitted to the existence of avian influenza and the EU officially criticised Thailand for the lack of transparency. Interestingly, Cambodia had already restricted Thai poultry exports weeks prior to the EU Commissioner's visit. Thailand did not only endanger the lives of its own people, but risked food safety concerns in other countries and played with the confidence of its biggest poultry market, the EU.

Vietnam has been similarly opaque in its reporting during the first few months of the outbreak, which started at the end of 2003. Epidemiologist Dr Richard Brown, head of a special outbreak response team, which has been set up jointly by the WHO and the Asian Development Bank, said to Agence France Press, "information sharing between the international community and the Vietnamese government has been less than satisfactory over the past month" (Agence France Press, 19 March 2004).

Avian influenza has been and continues to be a challenge for Southeast Asian states. The poultry industry lost billions in export and the governments incurred tremendous costs through compensation and vaccination schemes. Hundreds of people died in Southeast Asia. By 2007, Indonesia had the highest death toll in the world and the fatality rate was above 80 per cent. The death toll of Indonesia and Vietnam catapulted both countries on the top spots of the worst-affected countries in the world. On top of this, other NTS crises, including the Boxing Day Tsunami that was discussed in the Introduction, impeded the containment of the virus.

Interestingly, the avian influenza threat was not expedited by the Tsunami. For example it was first detected in Aceh nearly one year after the Tsunami. The virus has affected Southeast Asia unevenly. Some countries such as the insular Philippines were unaffected from the crisis. Nevertheless, regional cooperation was initiated, albeit delayed. It built on the previous SARS outbreak experience and designated support to the poorer countries that were affected by the outbreaks. Additionally, sub-regional and bilateral cooperative efforts were launched including the bilateral initiative to control the Thai–Malaysian border in 2004 or projects within the Ayeyawady-Chao Phraya-Mekong Economic Cooperation Strategy (ACMECS). Countries with greater resources and better infrastructure had a higher chance of rapid containment and recovery.

The EU's reaction and its initiatives

The EU took the avian influenza threat from Asia seriously. Firstly, the poultry imports posed a food safety threat to the people of the EU. Secondly, the migratory pattern of wild birds made avian influenza an immediate threat. Already in March 2003, the EU was facing the avian influenza threat from within and poultry was culled in the Netherlands, Belgium and Germany. Thus, the EU authorities were already highly sensitised when the disease broke out in Southeast Asia. They were very concerned about the high fatality and contagion rate of these outbreaks, as evident through Byrne's visit to Southeast Asia within a month after the first confirmed outbreak in Vietnam. The EU also participated in a meeting on global collaboration in combating avian influenza with the USA and twelve participating states from East Asia (Kyodo News, 28 January 2004).

In 2005, before the virus reached Europe, the EU revamped the Council Directive (92/40/EEC) on avian influenza to update the guidelines for the national plans. National contingency plans were set up. The closer the virus came, the greater was the construction of the threat by the media. Political debate on the topic enhanced and epistemic communities became more involved in shaping public threat constructions. Once cases were found in Turkey, the threat perceptions among the public heightened substantially, although European political leaders assured the public that European governments were prepared. In fact, when the virus struck on Western European soil in early 2006, political leaders expressed the outbreaks to be under control and urged the public to remain calm; French President Jacques Chirac demonstratively enjoyed eating chicken at an agricultural fair in Paris in February 2006. On the one hand, the EU and its member states were keen to securitise and derive policy implications for their own preparedness and safety. On the other, once the crisis reached Europe, some political leaders of poultry exporting countries reversed to de-securitisation to reassure the public and protect the domestic poultry industry.

Within the European Commission, DG for Health and Consumers Development was leading the intra-mural cooperation, whereas the external perspective was represented by DG RELEX coordinating with other DGs including DG Health, DG Development and DG Research. An array of avian influenza actions was pursued under various DGs, including DG Enlargement, to safeguard the EU beyond its borders. The EU issued trade restrictions and travel advisories. Europe was to be secured while, at the same time, it was expressed, *inter alia*, that the outbreak in Southeast Asia facilitated greater promotion of regional integration, sustainable development and democratisation. It provided an opportunity to increase and offer assistance that could create something more lasting (Maier-Knapp 2014: 227).

The activities of the EU focused on financial and technical support to selected Southeast Asian countries. A study on the relationship of gender and avian influenza in Laos, Vietnam and Thailand was commissioned and an EU experts delegation was sent to Vietnam. The financial assistance was mainly through the international Avian and Human Influenza Facility. This confirms the EU's adherence to the principle of multilateralism and the EU's interest in alleviating its administrative burden and ensuring aid effectiveness.

At the same time, bilateral initiatives of EU member states complemented European Commission assistance, whereupon there have been problems of coordination and resource duplication. European Commission officials stated that there is room for improvement in regard to coordination and information-sharing between the European Commission and the EU member states. It was argued that the European Commission informs the member states on a regular basis, but that vice versa the European Commission remains relatively uninformed and that "this is not an uncommon situation...and the UN would know more [than the European Commission]" (interview with EU official, 4 November 2009). There is an inherent political problem within the EU that is based on its multi-headed structure. Overlapping competences and inter-institutional rivalry complicate internal and external coordination and, hence, impact on the EU's external representation.

Within the ASEAN–EU Ministerial Meeting and ASEAN–EU JCC, avian influenza was not on the inter-regional agenda until 2007 and did not enjoy any form of threat prioritisation. Factually, the EU provided help commensurate with the scope of other external actors. Thus, when making claims about threat priorities, it is useful to put the EU's collective engagement into perspective and compare this with the activities of other external actors. The issue of avian influenza is a niche area and needs to be seen in the context of the overall ASEAN–EU relationship. While one may argue that greater regional and inter-regional cooperation and information-sharing could improve the overall preparedness of the Southeast Asian region and should be explored (Roy 2009), it is important to restate that the issue is a niche area, mainly addressed through sub-national, national and global fora.

Within ASEM, various workshops and seminars were organised from 2004 onwards (Maier-Knapp 2011a: 548). In 2009, the stockpile initiative was launched under the 9th ASEM Foreign Ministers' Meeting and provided 500,000 Tamiflu doses. This project also brought about the network of public health expertise. The development of ASEM's vaccine stockpile project is an interesting development, in the sense that it shows openness towards tangible cooperation among ASEM member states, moving beyond intangible commitments that are designed to respect the non-intrusion of domestic affairs. Generally speaking, ASEM initiatives have consisted mainly of a mix of state and non-state non-binding activities, disassociated from the practical implementation of pandemic security provided by ASEM member states. This ASEM stockpile project is innovative and suggests that ASEM may hold the potential to act as an umbrella framework for a variety of cooperative formations with regional and international organisations. Such multi-level cooperation within ASEM produces demand-oriented and tangible outcomes. It may be a new path for the more proactive and result-oriented ASEM member states to venture down. This indicates that ASEM's future role may be the role of an umbrella framework for pandemic preparedness, issue-specific governance and ad hoc forms of multi-level cooperation contributing to global governance.

Within the ARF, avian influenza has been on the agenda of security concerns from the 12th ARF Meeting onwards. The ministers expressed implications of avian influenza for regional security and highlighted the importance of national measures and the development of national preparedness plans (ASEAN member states 2005: para: 31). By the 16th ARF Meeting in 2009, the avian influenza threat was off the agenda. The ARF chairman's statements between 2005 and 2009 reaffirmed that this form of influenza is a serious NTS threat to the region and that there is a necessity for the ARF to respond in a comprehensive manner. Information-sharing on avian influenza was the main strategy that was promoted and there was only one official ARF initiative in this respect: Seminar on the Role of Military and Civil Cooperation in the Prevention and Control of the Spread of Communicable Diseases Such as SARS and Avian Influenza, in

Hanoi from 14 to 15 September 2005. These various initiatives within the ASEAN–EU dialogue, ASEM and the ARF involved the EU directly and indirectly. Thus, we could perceive the EU as an actor in accordance with the definition of an actor provided in Chapter 1.

Keeping with the important role of non-state actors, as described in the previous chapter, there were non-state actors that shared European behavioural standards to the poultry industry in Southeast Asian countries. These actors have been applying and transferring European standards through development cooperation to various agricultural, horticultural and aquacultural sectors for a long time. Avian influenza acted as a catalyst to enhance these efforts.

> Some success may be accounted for within the reformulation of regulatory standards in the poultry industry, although market and governmental pressure on the industry to reform may have been the main stimulus for the changes. Such initiatives comprising of local and foreign staff sharing their expertise in accordance to Western standards has definitely influenced change on the macro-level (policy-making and industry), but, on the micro-level, there has been insignificant behavioural and normative impact to suggest a cultural change of rural famers.
>
> (Maier-Knapp 2011a: 550–551)

In light of the tradition of backyard-farming within the majority of Southeast Asian countries, tackling the avian influenza threat requires change beyond the policy level. This cultural issue of the threat has been outlined even by the WHO on 21 September 2005. WHO demanded that Asia change its age-old farming practices to reduce contact between people and poultry to limit avian influenza and limit new animal diseases infecting humans (Reuters, 21 September 2005). This perspective was echoed within some ASEAN countries, which are attempting to alter these farming practices. Former Thai Agriculture Ministry official Nirandorn Uangtrakulsook observed that Southeast Asian countries are aiming to change the way poultry farming is done, but they are facing obstacles; he said, in Thailand, "10,000 farms, mostly small and medium sized, have not made upgrades despite the offer of low-interest loans through state-owned banks. Many farmers complain they don't have enough collateral" (Reuters AlertNet, 11 October 2005).

The case of the avian influenza outbreak in Southeast Asia has shown that the EU possessed issue-specific expertise, financial capacity and the goodwill to project its level of preparedness to other regions. The diverging threat perceptions, the patchy nature of the crisis, the lesser regional cohesion and openness in the counterpart region determined the EU's engagement.

This case study further displayed that trade interdependence has activated European interest to protect its consumers. The self-protective measures such as the poultry ban suggest that immediate EU actions in Southeast Asia need to be seen through a securitised lens and considered as precautionary assistance. The highly sensitised domestic context in the aftermath of the EU intra-regional avian influenza outbreaks of 2003 support the claim that EU engagement draws upon the technology of securitisation and should be considered as the continuation of domestic NTS concerns.

Conclusions

Through the case of the Bali Bombings and the avian influenza outbreak, this chapter illustrated that the security perspective towards Southeast Asia has been gaining greater prominence among the EU and its member states. The ASEAN region is no longer solely viewed through the developmental prism. The intra-regional integrative dynamics of CSDP and the September 11 attacks have added to this collective external security perspective in the early 2000s. They have strengthened an understanding and self-understanding of the EU as a collective actor which should act and be perceived as an NTS actor in the world.

Throughout this chapter, the EU and its member states have placed emphasis on the security-development nexus in their development of responsive action. Whereas the case of the Bali Bombings demonstrated that the collective perspective and competency was limited to addressing the underlying, long-term and socio-economic concerns, the case of avian influenza revealed collective securitisation efforts.

In accordance with the confined competency of the European Commission in the field of counter-terrorism, EU region-to-state and region-to-region activities focused on counter-terrorist-related activities. EU member state actions superseded the communitarian approach, but were lacklustre in comparison to the engagement of other international actors. They varied and were dependent on the threat perceptions, as well as the historical ties to the region. In the case of the avian influenza outbreak, EU activities appeared driven by perceptions of risk and socio-economic insecurity.

At the same time, this chapter demonstrated that the issue of inter-institutional coordination persists. Greater coherency and streamlining of threat perceptions to better dovetail EU supranational and member state actions on the operational level is urgently needed. At the same time, in instances of common threat perceptions activities on the various levels need to be transparent and improved in coordination. While the EU holds a comparative advantage over other actors in supporting ASEAN regional efforts in managing NTS challenges, it could not promote effectively this method in the case studies in light of various pre-conditions ranging from the uneven degree of affectedness among ASEAN member states to the lack of an appropriate regional counterpart for implementation. Finally, one also needs to note that sometimes the EU's actions obfuscate its moral high ground and raise questions about the EU as a normative actor in international affairs.

Notes

1 Al-Qaeda emerged at the end of the Cold War to continue the work of the Afghan *mujahidin* providing training of recruits and financial, ideological and operational support to Islamist terrorist groups throughout the world. In Southeast Asia, the organisation has been linked to local separatist and ethno-nationalist groups such as the Moro Islamic Liberation Front and the Abu Sayyaf Group in the Philippines, Lashkar Jundullah in Indonesia, Kumpulan Mujahidin Malaysia in Malaysia, Jemmah Salafiyah in Thailand, Arakan Rohingya Nationalist Organisation and Rohingya Solidarity Organisation in Myanmar, as well as JI.
2 US military clashes with Libya over Libya's territorial claims in the Gulf of Sidra in the 1970s and 1980s fuelled the anti-Americanism within the Arab world. Libya's revenge was in the form of international terrorism, which was primarily directed against the USA.
3 Please read, for instance, Javier Solana's press statement or the Council's conclusions on the terrorist attacks in Bali in October 2002.

5   The Aceh Monitoring Mission

In 2005, Katzenstein observed that "Asian states view human rights and election-watch commissions as unacceptable intrusions into their domestic affairs" (Katzenstein 2005: 141). In the very same year that Katzenstein published this observation, its truth was tested through the work of the AMM and the pursuant EU Election Observation Mission of the European Commission in Indonesia. The AMM aimed to implement peace in Aceh, which had been suffering from a political conflict for over thirty years.

The political conflict was triggered by a long series of domestic developments that had given economic and political concentration of power to Jakarta, and disadvantaged and deprived the Acehnese of their autonomy, fuelling anti-Javanese sentiments in the region. Sukarno's reign from 1945–1967 initially aimed for a secular and federalist nation-building process. However, this was dismissed by Sukarno himself in 1950 in favour of a secular and centralised process. This led to discontent among the Acehnese and the populations of some of the other provinces of Indonesia. The planned incorporation of Aceh into North Sumatra in 1951 led to the Acehnese joining the wider Islamist rebellion movement of Darul Islam from 1953 to 1962 (Braud and Grevi 2005: 9).

The GoI promised special status to Aceh in 1957 to resolve the problem. On the political and religious level, Jakarta ensured that the local elite of Aceh, the *ulamas*, supported the capital. They were embedded in Jakarta's religious network as part of an *ulama* national council structure (Braud and Grevi 2005: 10). The centre–periphery gap was widened by selective filling of the local administrative positions by non-Acehnese. In addition to this, those Acehnese, who were part of the political elite, were attracted by the possibility of affluence and power when they implemented government policies from Jakarta.

Under Suharto, the New Order regime continued on the path of centralisation and political, religious, educational, economic and cultural paternalism, but on a greater scale, including violent suppression of dissent[1].

The discovery of natural gas reserves within Acehnese territory in 1971 shifted the focal point of discrimination from the political to the economic sector and, consequently, led to further tensions within society. The industrialisation of Aceh brought profound change to the social structure and raised more resentments towards GoI among the Acehnese population. The people of Aceh have suffered the most from GoI's radical industrialisation course involving land eviction and migratory programmes of predominantly Javanese manpower into Aceh (Braud and Grevi 2005: 11–12). The aims of GoI were focused on maximising revenue and creating an infrastructure to achieve and sustain this. The Acehnese and the peoples of other peripheral provinces felt patronised and exploited.

In 1976, Hasan di Tiro and a group of Acehnese intellectuals founded the Free Aceh Movement (GAM). In contrast to Darul Islam, the GAM movement then known as the Aceh-Sumatra National Liberation Front was localised to Aceh. It was sustained by an elitist group on a small scale that was not aiming for an Islamic Indonesia but demanded an independent Aceh. Security forces crushed the movement from 1977 onwards, so that by 1979 the ideological leaders went into exile to Sweden. The middle-ranked and operational leaders of GAM as well as the foot soldiers fled into the remote and mountainous areas of Aceh. In spite of this setback, the ideological leaders managed to continue their propaganda campaign from abroad.

From 1989 to 1998 the Indonesian security forces launched a military offensive, the Daerah Operasi Militer (DOM). Aceh was declared a military operation zone. In 1990, the Jaring Merah counterinsurgency operations began wiping out GAM but within a year GAM reappeared. The DOM experience lasted nearly a decade and created a breeding ground for a radical generation of GAM combatants to emerge. Many of these combatants had been scarred by DOM and their number quintupled by the new millennium. GAM became a popular movement which expanded its geographical outreach immediately after the end of Suharto's regime.

The expansion from 1999 to 2000 was paired with an escalation in violence. In 2000 alone, approximately 1,000 people were killed in relation to the political conflict. This death toll in a single year matched that of the entire period of 1977–1995. While the GAM leadership was striving to internationalise the conflict, GAM's base was increasing its acts of terrorism. The case of East Timor's independence showed GAM's ideological leadership quite plainly that internationalising the Aceh conflict could be favourable for Acehnese independence.

Prior to the EU's involvement in 2005, there had been several other foreign attempts to end the conflict. In spite of the failure of previous peace talks and the pacifying attempts of external non-state actors, these past experiences of failure provided a more positive and open environment for the EU and ASEAN to operate in. On the one hand, the EU's engagement was not completely unfamiliar and on the other, a culture of peace had already been instilled to a minor degree. For example in 2001 and 2002, the Henri-Dunant Centre managed to achieve ceasefires, but these ceasefires were brittle, and could not work since they lacked the genuine support of the antagonists. Furthermore, the ASEAN member states, which acted as monitors, appeared to tolerate the military's hard line and could not prevent the two sides from clashing and committing atrocities.

As mentioned in the previous chapter, the September 11 attacks and the War on Terror campaign by the USA had an impact on Southeast Asia. The USA largely viewed Southeast Asia as the Second Front. This played into the hands of many Southeast Asian governments and provided a legitimate base for Indonesia to continue cracking down on GAM, despite lacking evidence to connect GAM with JI or international terrorism, namely al-Qaeda.[2] This is not to say that the conflict did not have a regional dimension. The conflict has been geographically confined to Indonesia, but has had some impacts in Thailand, Malaysia and the Malacca Straits through small arms trade and piracy attacks used as a source of income for GAM. To what degree the AMM exactly contributed to the decline in piracy is difficult to assess because of the criminalisation of GAM by the Indonesian Government, resulting in difficulty in differentiating between free-riders, splinter groups and actual GAM piracy (Sukma 2004). The better preparedness and coordination among the littoral ASEAN states effectively reduced the number of piracy cases. For example, this was achieved through the trilateral cooperation known as the Eye in the Sky initiative on maritime security in the Malacca Straits, raising the question of how to quantify the actual success of the AMM in relation to piracy. Organised crime in the form of illegal small arms shipments out of Thailand and financial support by Malaysian sympathisers could be interpreted as the transnationalisation of the conflict in the broadest sense and may have provided a convenient pretext for Indonesian authorities to assume a hard-line approach.

Overall, after Suharto, Jakarta's policy towards Aceh seemed inconsistent and confused by a variety of elements that foremost reflected the civil-military power struggle in Jakarta (Braud and Grevi 2005: 17). In May 2003, President Megawati Sukarnoputri imposed martial law on Aceh and declared a military emergency for a six-month period after GAM failed to accept the Special Autonomy offer issued by the Indonesian government. A large-scale offensive was launched against GAM. Once again, it seemed as if the rebel movement had been effectively wiped out. A year later the military emergency was downgraded to civilian emergency and another year later the civilian emergency was lifted.

The AFC in 1997/98 and the tsunami in 2004 occurred while there was conflict in Aceh. They had spill-over effects into the course of the conflict, re-orienting the focus of the security referent, as evident through GAM's leadership which stated in January 2005 that it does not intend to harm foreign aid workers. However, the excessive presence of foreign aid workers and military forces heightened the tensity within Muslim Aceh. Both NTS crises reminded Indonesia of the human plight and the individual in society as the main victim. For two decisive moments in history the traditional view of the state as being Indonesia's main security referent and guarantor was temporarily perverted. The AFC had negative effects on Indonesian politics and led to the end of Suharto's regime, indirectly influencing the new moderate policy orientation towards GAM, as well as GAM's increased openness towards ceasefire negotiations. The new government was more willing to engage in dialogue with the GAM. However, by 2003, the approach changed and the government declared a military emergency to eradicate GAM once and for all. At the end of 2004, the tsunami exacerbated the crisis in Aceh and allowed external influence into the region.

The peace process

After the tsunami, the EU became actively engaged in the crisis management and peace process in Aceh. The Crisis Management Initiative (CMI) and GoI were in contact about solving the conflict in Aceh before the tsunami struck (Gorman and Kivimäki 2008: 10). After the catastrophe, the connections were given a new impetus and funds were made available by the European Commission to support the GAM–GoI mediation process.

Following the mediation process, the Memorandum of Understanding (MoU) was brokered by Martti Ahtisaari and the CMI, and agreed on by the GAM and the GoI on 15 August 2005. The MoU is the heart of the operation. Once it was accepted and ratified by the parties in all its aspects (self-government, political participation, economic arrangements, security arrangements and amnesty) after six months of negotiation, the operational task of implementing was discussed in depth. An AMM official elaborated,

> The negotiations were ongoing in Helsinki in the first part of 2005 and during the negotiations the question came up as who would monitor any agreement that was reached between the parties. The UN was a

non-starter. There was no way the UN would get called in to monitor after what had happened in East Timor.

(interview with AMM official, 10 February 2009)

The UN, the USA and Australia have made a negative impression on Indonesia in the past. Furthermore, the ASEAN states failed to manage the preceding ceasefires. As indicated above, the case of the ASEAN monitors and peace-keepers was problematic. They lacked credibility, because they were accused by GAM of acting in favour of the Indonesian state. Moreover, peace-keepers from ASEAN member states are considered as fellows as well as regional competitors at the same time, complicating information flow and collaborative efforts.

Indonesia post-tsunami experienced an unforeseen surge of foreign assistance and presence, facilitating a certain basis of trust towards European actors. The poor infrastructure and lack of institutions to effectively coordinate and distribute aid in a vast archipelagic terrain, necessitated this opening. The post-Suharto democratisation process from within also added to this openness towards material and ideational influx from the West. Additionally, one needs to point out that the MoU clearly outlined the tasks and predefined the scope of the AMM. These preconditions meant that the EU was the most plausible and well-equipped option.

During the negotiations, GoI consented to Ahtisaari's proposal to invite the EU to monitor the peace process. The peace agreement was not yet established, but already, at the end of June, the EU had sent a team of experts to Indonesia to research the feasibility of a mission in Aceh. This was consented to by GoI. In July, GoI was encouraged by the EU to invite two non-EU countries and five ASEAN member states to participate in the monitoring mission. In Jakarta, the European side met with GoI and the ASEAN member states to discuss their contribution of 20 staff each. From 15 August until 15 September 2005, an Initial Monitoring Presence (IMP) bridged the gap from the ceasefire to the commencement date of the mission. The IMP was financed by bilateral contributions from CSDP member states. On 9 September 2005 the Council adopted the joint action on AMM and specified the mandate as follows:

(a) monitor the demobilisation of GAM monitor and assist with the decommissioning and destruction of its weapons ammunition, and explosives;
(b) monitor the relocation of non-organic military forces and non-organic police troops;
(c) monitor the reintegration of active GAM members;

(d) monitor the human rights situation and provide assistance in this field in the context of the tasks set out in points (a), (b) and (c) above;
(e) monitor the process of legislation change;
(f) rule on disputed amnesty cases;
(g) investigate and rule on complaints and alleged violations of the MoU;
(h) establish and maintain liaison and good cooperation with the parties
(Council of the European Union 2006a)

The Planning Team was given the task to design an Operation Plan (OPLAN) to be approved by the Council for the execution of the mandate on site. This decision was made based on the Technical Assessment Mission (TAM). There was some lack of clarity about the budget prior to the mission, however, a European presence was necessary in order to ensure the launch of AMM. Thus, the TAM and IMP staff had to improvise (Braud and Grevi 2005: 24).

The IMP had already been present in Aceh since 2 August 2005. On 18 July 2005, DG RELEX presented a work in progress document that specified the ways AMM could be financed. The timeline available for the financing process was limited and on 18 July 2005 after the General Affairs and External Relations Council conclusions, it was also clear that for the mission to be launched on 15 August 2005 would be cumbersome and the question about financing the process would very likely not yield any outcome soon (Braud and Grevi 2005: 22). In addition to this, it was the summer break in Brussels. The DG RELEX document led to a dispute that revolved around the legal obligations and competencies of the European Commission and the European Council.

> The question of financing ESDP operations is directly related to the exercise of political control and strategic direction on the mission itself. This is the reason why some Member States felt that, had its proposal been accepted, the Commission would have acquired excessive political influence on the running of the operation.... [T]he Council Legal Service submitted its opinion on the proposal of the Commission, and rejected it on legal, budgetary and political/institutional grounds. From a legal standpoint, it was argued that the RRM and the [Asia and Latin America] programme could not finance a crisis management operation pertaining to CFSP objectives.
> (Braud and Grevi 2005: 25)

These budgetary squabbles and the reluctance of some member states to get engaged in Aceh, required Solana's "assertive intervention" (Braud and Grevi 2005: 25). On 26 July 2005, Solana and Ahtisaari addressed the Political and Security Committee. The EU's ownership of the AMM was confirmed and the financing technicalities assigned to CFSP. Solana's intervention, however, did not necessarily resolve the budgetary issues in practice, but it clarified the competencies of the multiple bodies within the EU.

The AMM illustrates the necessity of adapting and transforming such cumbersome procedures and introducing new mechanisms to advance CSDP responses of high urgency and avoid financial dependency on the goodwill of individual states. A failure of the AMM during the implementation phase would have probably not singled out the institutional shortcomings in such a pronounced manner, since the financial mechanisms have worked very well in other cases. A failure of the AMM on operational grounds would have probably completely distracted from the financing squabbles prior to the deployment.

In general, the EU and its member states have market concerns as the most important variable when deciding on a specific action. They are in a zone of peace where economic well-being is the main objective of political survival, and now even more so. This rationale is one out of many features that distinguishes the EU and other Western political entities from developing ASEAN member states, which are living in a tense regional environment against the backdrop of the Great Power Rivalry and the necessity for many states to develop stable and mature statehood. This rationale is further complicated by the diversity of domestic cultures and interests of the member states.

In the case of Aceh, it was mainly the Nordic countries which persuaded sceptical fellow member states to consent to an engagement in a remote area. For example, Sweden, previously mentioned as being the place of exile for the GAM leadership, pushed and argued on the basis of humanitarian grounds in favour of the AMM. The main challenge for the other countries was how to overcome the domestic and near-neighbourhood focus of their policy-making rationale. How could they accommodate domestic cost-benefit priorities, while providing resources to a mission for a greater global good?

Six days after the Council's decision on OPLAN, the European Commission's decision was made and the AMM was given a budget of €9.3 million from the EU and €6 million by the participating states and EU member states (Aceh Monitoring Mission 2005). Within a limited timeframe of two months the EU has managed to draw up an operational plan, organise the staff and come up with a budget.

On 15 September 2005 the AMM was launched in Aceh. The EU and ASEAN teams started the AMM by monitoring the decommissioning of weapons on the GAM side and the withdrawal of the government's troops out of the region. Justin Davies, Head of Staff of the AMM, said that, at the launch of the mission, there were some concerns about whether any GAM rebels would show up in the stadium where they had organised the first decommissioning of GAM weapons (interview with AMM official, 10 February 2009). According to the interviewed AMM personnel and EU practitioners, it appears that beyond this concern, all other aspects of the mandate were fulfilled to the EU's and GoI's satisfaction. On 15 December 2006, the AMM mandate to assist and monitor the peace process was completed.

In addition to the AMM, the European Commission drew up long-term and flanking projects. Following the deployment of the AMM, the European Commission came up with a support package of €8.5 million to help reintegrate former combatants and amnestied prisoners (EU Delegation to Indonesia and Brunei Darussalam 2009). Furthermore, it allocated €15.85 million for the organisation of the local election in 2006 and reform of the police and jurisdiction, as well as the re-establishment and reform of the public sector (EU Delegation to Indonesia and Brunei Darussalam 2009).

"Success has many fathers"

Despite the CSDP's ownership of the AMM, the ongoing peace emphasises the complementary approaches of the multiple heads within the EU in specific crisis management situations. In order to establish permanent peace in conflict situations, there is a clear difference in approach and competency towards crisis and conflict management between the European Commission and the European Council. In simplified terms, the European Council pursues a military and security approach, whereas the European Commission is more concerned with the long-term dimension of establishing peace. The European Commission seems to focus on structural projects, for instance, rule of law and capacity-building in the public sector. This is not to deny that the European Council does not outline structural objectives and guidelines. There are grey areas, which should nevertheless not deflect from the fact that the long-term, structural, ideological and cultural objectives are to be found in the majority of initiatives by the European Commission in an operational manner.

One European Commission official explained that the success of the AMM and the ongoing peace are the results of two complementary methods for the implementation of peace. That is, the AMM is supported by projects of the European Commission that aim for the improvement of the structural settings. In this context, he added that "[w]ith a security approach you can win the war but not the peace" (interview with EU official, 5 February

2009). He clarified this division of labour in the metaphor of the European Commission being the 'software' and the CSDP being the 'hardware'. The main purpose of the AMM was to safeguard an unproblematic transition from an unstable and violent situation to a situation of peace where human rights and the rule of law can be implemented.

According to the head of the TAM, from the outset of the AMM, "the mission was never in question because the EU knew they could do it" (interview with AMM official, 10 February 2009). The translation of the mandate to the operational level was the responsibility of Pieter Feith and his team of civilian crisis management experts. Their vision was of teams that were diverse in terms of gender and cultural background. The staff were a combination of experienced European experts who possessed knowledge on international crisis management, human rights and other technical expertise, while on the ASEAN side, there were staff with local knowledge and cultural awareness in a Muslim society. The mission consisted of a total of 220 staff. They were unarmed and trained for civilian crisis management.

During the TAM four ASEAN officers were involved. Davies said that they agreed to the EU's vision and "were quite happy to have the EU lead", and he further acknowledged that the mission "wouldn't have been as effective without the ASEAN side", because of their local and cultural know-how (interview with AMM official, 10 February 2009).

The history of the EU itself is a multicultural experience suggesting that the EU must be capable of conducting cross-cultural operations. Antje Wiener has argued that the EU's past has given it a highly differentiated pool of knowledge to draw upon and taught it to be a tolerant actor from within (Wiener 2008). Some national incidents such as the controversy of the burqa ban in France suggest that such claims need to be differentiated and that there is a difference between the supranational and domestic level.

While the interviewed AMM officials portrayed cultural issues to have had minimal impact on the functioning of the teams, Kirsten Schulze has been more critical of the AMM's neglect of the cultural dimension. The limited timeframe for drafting the mission resulted in the lack of language training and organisation of qualified interpreters (Schulze 2007: 5). In fact, Davies admitted that there were language and cultural differences, but these obstacles did not interfere with the smooth running of the operation (interview with AMM official, 10 February 2009). Another aspect that intrigued Schulze was the AMM's "lack of focus on implementing the human rights elements at the beginning of the process, which made it possible for the AMM to ultimately complete its mission in the highly sensitive context of Indonesian domestic politics" (Schulze 2007: 14).

She stated that human rights lacked incorporation throughout the AMM process.

The MoU included various human rights clauses, but, in practice, these clauses seemed to have had very little influence as, for example, in the case of the Law on the Governance of Aceh (LoGA). The passing of the LoGA raised criticism from the European Parliament, GAM and international as well as local NGOs (Schulze 2007: 9–10). The LoGA was perceived as a central government legislation that neglected the dialogue with the Acehnese ethnic minority. Its incorporation of Sharia Law further raises questions about liberalisation and democratisation processes within Indonesia. International NGOs pointed out that the document fell short in guaranteeing minority rights, religious freedom, freedom of expression and gender equality (Schulze 2007: 10).

In particular, in view of the European Council's adoption of the UNSCR1325 in 2005, Schulze argued that the AMM was not in line with the EU's own standards. She raised a valid point, in light of Title V, Chapter 1, Art. 10a, and the various international conventions on human rights to which the EU and its member states are signatories. However, with regard to the AMM's specific task (d) on human rights, it was also evident that the focus of the human rights mandate was only in relation to points (a), (b) and (c). The AMM was concerned with monitoring human rights aspects revolving around decommissioning, withdrawal of GoI-associated troops, amnesty and reintegration of ex-GAM combatants. In reference to the interviews with the EU and AMM officials, any other form of human rights surveillance and intervention would have jeopardised the mission. "Let's say, it is not a contradiction in first place. It is a Realpolitik, a recognition of Realpolitik. You aim for goals. You have a certain vision....We thought human rights, democracy [etc.] are important" but "normative influence was limited from the outset notwithstanding a vision that we have" (interview with EU official, 5 February 2009).

EU officials have argued that CSDP staff were not in a position to promote human rights during the negotiations as well as the peace process since, first and foremost, it was Indonesia's problem and not the EU's problem. The EU was not actively negotiating in Helsinki and only consented to Ahtisaari as the mediator. Ahtisaari was paid by the EU but he did not represent the EU. He might have wanted a stronger focus on human rights during the process, but this was his personal ambition and not to be mistaken for the EU's official rhetoric (interview with EU official, 5 February 2009). The only dimension of the EU's engagement in Aceh which clearly supports a value-consistent picture of the EU as an actor was the long-term development assistance that had been in place for decades as part of the European Commission's and the individual EU member states' approach to Indonesia. This assistance is part of a greater European strategy facilitating and shaping the perception of the EU as an actor.

The success of the AMM brought along expectations towards the EU as an actor in the region. Southeast Asian officials frequently associate the EU with this peace-keeping and monitoring operation and have developed certain role expectations that have opened up avenues for potential future CSDP engagement in Mindanao and Southern Thailand. These role expectations compel the EU to analyse its success critically. The EU's monitoring role is now a major characteristic of the EU as security actor in Southeast Asia.

The EU is not interested in a military or strategic presence in the region like the USA and deems this economically unviable. Since the EU and the majority of its member states officially reject any deep strategic commitment to the region – with a few exceptions including the Five Power Defence Agreements between the UK and selected ASEAN states – European engagement has proven to be compatible with ASEAN's principle of non-interference. The EU's quick-in-and-out approach, once the AMM mandate ended, was regarded with favour and was a positive signal to Indonesia and ASEAN that the EU will not be intrusive and go beyond its mandate.

At the time of writing, the EU would like to retain a certain presence in Aceh, namely in the form of the Europa House. The EU believes that the reintegration and disbursement tasks of ex-combatants are still uncompleted. There are certain fears that an entire European withdrawal could allow tensions to rise again (interview with EU official, 27 May 2010). This extension of the presence of the Europa House is viewed with a degree of scepticism by Indonesian officials.

A concern that was raised on the European side by the head of TAM and IMP in the aftermath of the AMM was the lack of inter-regional follow-up building on the success of the AMM. He regarded the AMM as a missed opportunity to institutionalise something more lasting, such as an inter-regional crisis management mechanism that can be drawn upon in future scenarios to avoid the complex financing process. A senior advisor to the European Commission also expressed that the ASEAN side seemed marginally interested in establishing regular follow-up cooperation with CSDP (interview with EU official, 6 February 2009). In spite of these shortcomings, the AMM gave impetus that led to the Nuremberg Declaration, which stimulated a new dynamic within the ASEAN–EU Ministerial Meeting.

The CSDP's first mission to the region contributed to a positive image of the EU, but the reality of Southeast Asia is that peace-keeping actors attract limited interest in a region preoccupied with hard security. The case displayed the EU as capable of projecting capabilities to remote regions. It showed that European staff successfully planned and executed a programme that integrated the actors of the other region. It indicated the putative collective political willingness of the EU to act in Southeast Asia and fulfil its self-proclaimed role conception of a crisis manager abroad. For example, Benita Ferrero-Waldner has expressed this in a different context to the AMM, albeit inspired by the AMM and other ongoing CSDP missions.

> In our foreign policy we will prioritize conflict prevention and crisis management; promoting human rights and human security; and strengthening effective multilateralism.... We will continue to champion human rights and put particular emphasis on human security... responding to the full range of threats afflicting the most vulnerable in societies across the world, such as hunger, deadly diseases, environmental degradation and physical insecurity.
>
> (Ferrero-Waldner 2005)

Mainstreaming human rights into the implementation of the tasks of peacekeeping operations is a problem and it seems that "to champion human rights" might not have been adequately reflected within the AMM. The official tendency within the various CSDP documents to mainstream human rights and democratisation may pose problems for future CSDP engagement within the ASEAN region.

First and foremost, the AMM was a success story for GoI. The various stakeholders and influential figures on the EU and ASEAN side contributed to Aceh's peace. In the end, every side can claim to be part of this success. However, the following claims have proven to be overly optimistic. This may have been the result of a certain degree of post-mission euphoria on the European side.

> The EU, which has proved with AMM that it can considerably contribute to peace and stability in South East Asia, should build on the new political prestige in the region and will take steps towards enhancing both the EU–ASEAN relationship.[...] Moreover, COASI [Council Working Party on Asia-Oceania] concurs that AMM has given an important impetus to EU–ASEAN cooperation, as both the evaluation prepared by the AMM Chief of Staff and the comments by CIVCOM [Committee for Civilian Aspects of Crisis Management] underline. COASI noted and welcomed that the lessons learned are already being incorporated in the Action Plan to be adopted by the EU–ASEAN Ministerial meeting in March in Nuremberg. The EU is in the unique position to be able to contribute to this process by

offering ASEAN an opportunity to learn more about the ESDP, its structures and processes, with a view to fostering the development of capabilities and procedures appropriate for ASEAN-specific needs.
(Council of the European Union 2007)

This positive outlook did not end in concrete follow-ups in terms of enhanced security cooperation. The AMM has paved the way for future engagement of this type in the region. However, the positive image of the EU as an impartial and non-violent security actor which is welcomed again, may, in practice, counter the EU's normative identity. It may prove that certain core principles and values may be more difficult to translate into practice.

The EU as an actor and the question of normativity

The case of the AMM presents an instance where a remote crisis triggered EU action seemingly driven by altruism. Crisis situations automatically premise the goal or purpose and, thus, the formulation of these is obsolete. In the case of Aceh, the conflict-torn societies were additionally affected by a sudden natural catastrophe which deprived the people of their sources of livelihood. Overnight, Aceh became a matter of human survival. In a situation where the state is overburdened and unprepared, it will be more willing to let external actors in to help. These circumstances further facilitate the human security debate and thus, the human rights debate to sneak in. In such a vulnerable society, there is a greater chance for external actors to create space for discourse on contested norms and values as the faith of the crisis-ridden people in their own government is at a low-point. The UN Children's Fund (UNICEF) and other UN agencies, the International Committee of the Red Cross (ICRC), the Cooperative for Assistance and Relief Everywhere (CARE) and other international organisations provided humanitarian aid immediately after the Tsunami and, at the same time, they propagated human rights awareness (Jamil and Hersutanto 2007: 5).

The overall goal is simple; it is responding to a crisis to rescue lives and end human suffering. Yet, the overall goal or purpose is only the general rationale explaining the action. This needs to be further differentiated and it needs to be understood that the policy- and operation-related purposes substantiate the general goal. The interests and goals of the EU member states differed in the early stages of deciding on the AMM, but the EU's multiple heads appeared cohesive in the execution. The EU did not formulate the AMM goals as they were pre-defined by the GAM and GoI. In the end, the EU as a collective actor managed to produce a set of aggregated interests that could realise the MoU, despite various passive member states. The EU conceptualised OPLAN and implemented it. The case displayed the complexity of interest aggregation and development of action within the EU's complex policy-making structure and showed the EU as an important NTS actor in Southeast Asia.

Scholars such as Schulze have criticised the mission as having compromised EU values to some extent (Schulze 2007). The European Commission has attempted to compensate this shortcoming with its complementary engagement. The multiple heads of the EU that are involved in the EU's policy process enable the EU to be value- and identity-consistent through alternative paths. The EU's normative agenda raises questions of cooperative compatibility with Southeast Asia. Its quick-in-and-out approach make the EU a suitable partner for Southeast Asia, respecting ASEAN's principle of non-interference. The EU appears to be minimally invasive and open to being persuaded to tone down its normative expectations. It is not interested in a permanent military, strategic entanglement in the region and overall, it has proven to be compatible with ASEAN's principle of non-interference.

The AMM attests that the EU is capable of planning, deploying funds, resources and civilian manpower to a remote region and acting outside multilateral frameworks. The EU played a distinctive and significant role in overcoming the crisis. It took up the leadership role in monitoring and implementing the peace process. The EU was not merely one out of many contributors in alleviating or resolving the problem as it has been in the other chapters. It was an active, yet multi-headed actor, both strategiser and executor of the operational plan to manage the NTS challenge. It provided the overall strategy and operational plan for its partners and led the mission. The ASEAN partners played an important support role in executing the plan. The EU has proven that it can act as a coherent collectivity and overcome intra-regional issues of competency overlap and inter-institutional rivalry to effectively strategise, lead and delegate.

Furthermore, the AMM has proven that the circumvention of multilateral frameworks is necessary from time to time and that nevertheless the EU can live up to the global governance responsibility that falls on it. This does not mean that the EU only displays rhetorical commitment to multilateralism. The EU acts in accordance with the given situation. If an approach via an international organisation or a multilateral forum appears inappropriate, although these bodies may be better prepared or equipped to act, the EU will take responsibility, if this is mandated. This also depends on whether it views the problem as manageable and its actions as appropriate. The AMM boosted the EU's confidence. The rhetoric of EU foreign policy officials in the following years built on this success story to define the EU's role in Asia and the world. For instance, the following statement by Ferrero-Waldner in 2006 was inspired by the success of the AMM.

> The EU is the world's biggest donor, but we often lack the flexibility to move quickly. We will make crisis management a particular focus in the coming years, building on our strategy for disaster alert and preparedness. Our aim is to develop flexible and responsive solutions to crisis situations and so be a better partner for the military component of crisis response.
>
> (Ferrero-Waldner 2006)

Conclusively, despite the EU's clear and significant role in Aceh, the notion of the EU as a crisis manager in Southeast Asia does not appear to be a role conception inherent to the EU, yet. It seems that, at the present stage, the EU's NTS engagement in Southeast Asia is regularly perceived as sporadic cooperation. This satisfies the European public's humanitarian concerns, given that this public has normative expectations related to democracy, civil liberties and human rights. At the same time, it allows an incremental adaptation towards a more robust role that is still in tune with the opinion of the European public.

The EU is still seeking to establish its security role in Southeast Asia. The fact that the European Commission pushed for the AMM and that it initially aspired for greater involvement affirms that a young and non-state member of the international community like the EU may have considered this mission as a step towards greater recognition and parity of the EU as a collective international actor on politico-security matters. In this context William I. Zartman's description of humanitarian actors appears relevant to the EU's engagement in Aceh. He said,

> [a]ll non-state actors have an interest in enhancing their positions as useful third parties, not out of any venal egotism but because they believe they have something to offer; furthermore, a reinforcement of their standing and reputation helps them do their job.
>
> (Zartman 2008: 160)

Conclusions

This chapter elucidated the CSDP as an actor and displayed the process of how the AMM became operational. It illustrated the complex interplay of the EU's multiple heads and the identity conflict in regard to human rights during the implementation of the tasks. The European Commission provided financial assistance for the TAM and IMP, and CSDP was responsible for devising and implementing OPLAN. In addition to the AMM, the European Commission launched flanking projects. These were able to go beyond the MoU and address human rights and social issues directly and, therefore, uphold the EU's normative agenda.

CSDP's first action in the region contributed to a positive image of the EU as a collective security actor, but lacked follow-up. It showed that the EU as a collective actor can get its act together to make coherent decisions and deploy personnel on peace-keeping missions to Southeast Asia. At the same time, this case of NTS engagement raised concerns about the extent to which the EU adheres to its human rights rhetoric.

NTS challenges and EU engagement in Southeast Asia do not necessarily imply quick-fix pragmatism. They demand a nuanced and case-sensitive understanding. Evidently, the EU as a collective actor is aware of the opportunities and limitations of NTS challenges. The EU needs to be a competitive actor while being consistent with its identity. It still needs to figure out how to achieve its desire to become a power in the Asia-Pacific that is to be reckoned with.

Notes

1 General Suharto and his security forces established security and order through brutal anti-Communist and anti-separatist campaigns terrorising the country. Force was the first and only resort in his reign of terror, whereas in the first decade of Sukarno the military had not yet tightened its grip. There was still room for the Acehnese to negotiate with the government.
2 Libya has been the guerrilla warfare training ground for the second generation of GAM rebels, and therefore this raised allegations that GAM had links to international terrorism during the mid-1980s. However, this lacks evidence and logic in the context of international terrorist networks, including al-Qaeda. These connections would only apply to a small faction of GAM.

6 Non-traditional security crises since the Aceh Monitoring Mission

The years following the AMM saw the rising importance of the dialogue and cooperation on NTS challenges between ASEAN and the EU, interweaving political, security and socio-economic concerns on both sides. In 2008, a decade after the AFC, Southeast Asia witnessed many and diverse NTS challenges, reminiscent of the year 1998 when governments were toppled. The global economic and financial downturn, the soaring food prices culminating in the food riots across the Global South and the devastation caused by Cyclone Nargis in Myanmar re-raised concerns about ASEAN's stability. These issues revived the debate on NTS challenges and the need for effective regional cooperation.

Enhanced institutional proliferation and NTS threat-proofing on the domestic and regional levels have left many Southeast Asian countries prepared to safeguard their economies. Indeed, the global financial downturn seemingly spared the Asian economies. There were, however, NTS challenges, like the global food crisis in 2008, reminiscent of 1998 when food insecurity drove people onto the streets. The high fuel and commodity prices as well as the skyrocketing consumption were issues governments could not manage effectively. In the Philippines, armed troops had to monitor the sale of rice. In Indonesia, violence erupted and the country's socio-economic meltdown compelled Suharto to end his reign.

In April 2008, the situation in many Southeast Asian countries was similarly tense. The head of the UN World Food Programme even likened the soaring food prices to a "silent tsunami" (UN News Centre 2008).

> She said that like the 2004 tsunami, which hit the Indian Ocean leaving quarter of a million dead and about 10 million more destitute, the food price crisis – the biggest challenge WFP has faced in its 45-year history – requires a global response.

In April 2008, the supplier battle between Vietnam, Cambodia and Thailand sharpened and fuelled the already volatile and high rice prices, leading to low affordability and low rice imports within other Southeast Asian consumer countries. ASEAN governments reacted and reignited cooperation within the existing food security frameworks on the ASEAN and APT level, including the ASEAN Emergency Rice Reserve, ASEAN Food Security Reserve and the Food Information and Early Warning System.

The ASEAN Ministerial Meeting on Agriculture and Forestry was the main forum to address food security on the regional level. It discussed the ASEAN Integrated Food Security Framework in August 2008. This implied timely information-sharing and transparency on policy decisions, agricultural development plans and trade. This framework is supported by the Strategic Plan of Action on Food Security that considers food security and emergency relief, sustainability of food production, stronger food security information systems for monitoring and forecasting and agricultural innovation. ASEAN states committed to a sustainable and comprehensive approach to food security within the ASEAN and APT frameworks, which recognised the inter-relatedness of food and energy security.[1]

The EU and its member states followed with interest the unfolding events and the response of the ASEAN Secretariat and member states. The EU as an important importer of Southeast Asian foodstuffs would like to see Southeast Asia as a secure and safe supplier. Particularly, against the backdrop of the discussed case of the avian influenza outbreaks in the region and Thailand's concealment of affected poultry, EU authorities are keen to ensure food safety and assist in improving sanitary and phytosanitary standards in the region.

Given the global scale of the food crisis in 2008, European Council conclusions on food security in June 2008 received immediate attention and concerted realisation among the European Commission, Development Ministers and European Parliamentarians. In December 2008, the €1billion Food Facility was launched as the appropriate response to aid the developing countries. While African countries have been the main beneficiaries, there were small developing Southeast Asian economies like Laos which also received substantial assistance under this scheme. The EU offered international assistance and collaboration with UN agencies. Its immediate response to the crisis took place on the global level.

In the following years, the EU drew on existing dialogue mechanisms within the ASEAN–EU dialogue, including the biannual Indicative Lists of Activities, READI and the most recent Bandar Seri Begawan Plan of Action among others to complement wider global development frameworks. European support to Southeast Asia aims at devising new initiatives that promote sustainable food security, for instance, through the ASEAN–EU Science, Technology and Innovation initiative of 2012 or the EU Food-for-Assets project. Most importantly, the EU and its member states are committed to strengthening the ASEAN integrated regional food security frameworks. European Council President Herman van Rompuy stated,

> The EU and ASEAN countries have long realised the importance of food security in their bilateral relationship, all the more so since the food shortages of 2008.
>
> Currently, the EU has major programmes in Burma/Myanmar, Cambodia, and Laos to help eradicate extreme poverty and hunger. It is estimated that in Cambodia alone, more than 700 000 people have directly benefited from EU funded food security projects in a period of 7 years (2003–2009). Activities range from improving practices in agriculture, forestry and fisheries, to ensuring better maternal and child health care and increasing access to clean water and sanitation.
> (European Council President, 8 November 2011: 3)

The global food security debate has also stimulated greater intra-regional debate within the EU on the Common Agricultural Policy and the need for Europe to guarantee its own sustainable food supply. In addition to this debate, the EU and its member states have been facing criticism on the EU's biofuel subsidies and the impact that these have had on farming and plantation practices in developing countries. This affected many Southeast Asian countries, which have experienced a significant agricultural transformation to large-scale monocultures aimed at delivering crops for biofuel production. One could argue that the EU's interest in energy security and climate change appears to conflict with the MDG of fighting hunger. Generally speaking, this implies that the EU as an actor on NTS challenges in Southeast Asia needs to approach NTS issues in a holistic and sustainable manner, recognising the correlation and confinements of the individual sectors and issues of governance. This may require increasing expertise-based and functional region-to-region cooperation.

On 2 and 3 May 2008, severe storms of over 200 km/h swept over the Irrawaddy delta. Cyclone Nargis devastated the region and sharpened the food crisis in Myanmar. It destroyed livelihoods and infrastructure and affected millions of people and killed over 80,000 in Myanmar. Despite the devastation, the military junta initially denied foreign assistance and did not respond immediately with relief efforts. The EU, spearheaded by the Big Three, claimed that Myanmar's government failed to protect and act in the interest of its population. French Foreign Minister Bernard Kouchner sought to bring this "crime against humanity" to the UN as a case for the employment of the Responsibility to Protect principle. Unsurprisingly, this sweeping interpretation of the principle faced objection from many non-Western states.

The days passed by and the military junta was slow to issue visas for foreign assistance specialists and allow limited international access by the UN and individual "friendly" countries, including Thailand and Italy (Selth 2008: 388). ASEAN continued negotiating for greater humanitarian access and was integral in persuading Myanmar to set up an aid coordinating facility with ASEAN and the UN, known as the Tripartite Core Group to ensure access and recovery efforts.

The European Commission and EU member states provided significant financial assistance and Brussels has been actively encouraging the military junta to be more open-minded and understanding (Boisseau du Rocher 2012: 173). However, European disaster relief assistance in Myanmar did not provide a stepping stone for greater engagement. It did not soften the official European position towards Myanmar. In fact, in light of the fraudulent constitutional referendum in the aftermath of Cyclone Nargis, the EU and its member states have criticised the constitution's drafting as well as the referendum process. In late April 2008, in response to the lack of civilian input into the constitution's drafting, the EU under the Slovenian Presidency further restricted its sanctions regime towards Myanmar (Agence France Press, 23 April 2008). Clara Portela and Marco Bünte have suggested,

> The range of sanctions imposed against Myanmar by the EU since 1991 is a heterogeneous mix. These sanctions did not result from a predesigned plan, but were rather wielded gradually and articulated in accordance with the impulses provided by a series of civil society campaigns.
>
> (Bünte and Portela 2012: 4)

While there is the recognition that the policy of sanctions has not yielded the desired effect, the EU's official rhetoric has changed only very slowly. The EU's political approach to Myanmar did not change in the aftermath of Cyclone Nargis; however, European actors displayed immediate willingness to assist the people of Myanmar. Overall, the year 2008 marked a rise in humanitarian contributions by the EU to Southeast Asia, particularly to Myanmar, affirming this book's basal assumption that crises enhance interaction.

At the same time, this crisis demonstrated to the EU that its official sanction-based approach lacked teeth and that the military junta will not give in to external pressure. Interestingly, in spite of an increase in aid volume to the region, the EU's political perspective and sanction-based approach further consolidated. We can even argue that this crisis sharpened and contrasted the different ASEAN and EU normative principles such as the position of some EU member states in favour of the invocation of the Responsibility to Protect principle demonstrated. Following the political opening in Myanmar since early 2011, the EU finally suspended its sanctions in April 2012, with the exception of the arms embargo.

Another significant test for Southeast Asian regional cohesion through an NTS challenge was in 2009. Swine flu broke out in Mexico and was declared a global pandemic. Building on previous experiences of the SARS and avian influenza outbreaks, Southeast Asian governments activated regional and international mechanisms. Under the umbrella of ASEM, antivirals had been stockpiled in Singapore and distributed to ASEAN member states. The swine flu tested the EU's and ASEAN's regional frameworks of pandemic preparedness. The ASEAN–EU level acknowledged the threat of swine flu and the importance of global, regional and national structures in coping with this NTS threat.

At the 17th AEMM in 2009 in Cambodia, the keynote address by Deputy Prime Minister Hor Namhong highlighted the capacity-building and best-practice-sharing efforts of ASEAN and EU in NTS areas of human smuggling, drug trafficking, illicit trade and circulation of small arms and light weapons, anti-money laundering, international economic and cyber crimes. He further focused his attention on the recent swine flu outbreak and suggested,

> The swine flu is just one of the global infectious diseases that we need to actively promote our closer cooperation. We should not wait until such an outbreak of infectious disease. Instead, we should enhance our collaboration within the region, and certainly between the regions, such as ASEAN and the EU, to ensure that we can respond more effectively to the outbreak of any infectious diseases, such as this swine flu, Avian Influenza, and so forth.
>
> (Deputy Prime Minister of Cambodia 2009: 3)

In 2009, parallel to the swine flu concern, the EU has been preoccupied with tackling the NTS issue of piracy in the Gulf of Aden. Since the end of 2008, the EU has sought to protect European vessels through Operation Atalanta. It aimed to deter and, when necessary, use active force. The EU has expressed its interest in sharing its anti-piracy experience in the Gulf of Aden with Southeast Asia to contribute to the management of piracy issues in the Malacca Strait, in particular. Among others, CSDP

EU Military Committee chairman offered this in 2009 in his visit to the ASEAN Secretariat, alongside greater dialogue on disaster relief and non-proliferation. In 2012, Operation Atalanta was complemented by EU Nestor in the Horn of Africa. This mission focuses on regional capacity-building to tackle the piracy issue.

The EU is recognised as an important economic power in Southeast Asia, and now, it is delving increasingly into avenues of security cooperation to expand its profile as an actor. Amid the eurozone crisis, the EU has become more aware of the utility of its broad range of capacities ideal for addressing the panoply of NTS challenges. Some EU member states, as well as their defence industries, are placing greater emphasis on intertwining the economic and security perspectives. Prior to the eurozone crisis, the lack of domestic stimulus and the normative constraints to engage with Southeast Asia, defined the EU's low security perspective on the region. Concurrently, NTS challenges provide an avenue to make use of domestic crisis constructions and modify Europe's international role to suit the contemporary EU in the world.

In particular, the peace-building success of the AMM has been a stepping stone facilitating the EU's expansion of its international profile and consolidating the EU's security perspective to Asia. In fact, decades of assistance in conflict situations in Southeast Asia have created an environment conducive to greater European involvement in this area. For many decades, the EC has been engaged in the Philippines and rated its engagement there as successful (Dosch et al. 2011). In 1988, EC assistance commenced in the agricultural realm and gradually extended to other sectors, including confidence- and peace-building in Mindanao. The EU and its member states have contributed significantly to the peace process in Mindanao through the Mindanao Trust Fund, UN and various NGOs to support the civilian victims of this half-a-century-long conflict. In 2008, an IfS grant of €1 million was launched to support the work of three NGOs in assisting with the peace dialogues between the government and the insurgency groups, civil society confidence-building efforts, human rights monitoring, early warning and various grassroots activities. In 2010, a second IfS grant was released to continue the peace-supporting partnerships of the EU. In parallel to this financial assistance, the EU committed to continuous humanitarian assistance even during periods of extreme violent conflict.

In light of the EU's long-standing development and humanitarian involvement in the province, parties to the conflict expressed trust in the EU and were favourable towards an integral role of the EU in the peace-building efforts (MacDonald and Vinals 2012: 24). Namely, the UK became an active member of the International Contact Group, formatted to resolve the Mindanao issue in collaboration with the local parties to the conflict. The International Contact Group showed interest in the European Commission's support to Mindanao and invited the EU to share its experience.

Similarly, the EU's and its member states' engagement in Southern Thailand has provided a good foundation of trust. This engagement has given the impression that the EU is a low-intrusive and human-development-oriented assistance provider which takes genuine interest in contributing to the peace of the inter-ethnic conflict stemming from the annexation of the southern provinces by Thailand in 1902. In the last decade, violence in Southern Thailand has been a constant. Various attempts of the military, civilian government, royal family and international actors to stop the terror in the four most southern provinces of Thailand have failed to reach any significant breakthrough.

The EU and its member states have followed the developments in Southern Thailand cautiously, aware that this is Thailand's own internal affair, despite potential instability spilling over to the wider region (Kiatpongsarn 2011: 95–96). They have offered assistance to the Thai authorities and made available considerable financial resources, channelled to local NGOs and European organisations, including the Konrad-Adenauer Stiftung and the German–Southeast Asian Centre of Excellence for Public Policy and Good Governance based at Thammasat University in Bangkok. The financial support facilitated the sustenance of legal aid centres, greater media coverage, seminars or workshops on human rights, legal access and gender equality, internship programs for students and various other projects. Southern Thailand also received IfS grants to support confidence-building and reconciliation.

The European Commission's understanding of security is increasingly taking note of violent security conflicts in regions far away. The employment of the IfS in these instances suggests that development and humanitarian assistance has facilitated a collective international politico-security profile. This should not necessarily be interpreted in an evolutionary sense. Rather, it should be seen as an attempt of the European Commission to bridge the development and security divide within the EU structure itself. Since the EU as a collective actor does not act in a regulatory manner in its external relations, the relations with faraway regions provide a convenient platform for the EU to develop its international presence actively. This takes place seemingly with the domestic support of the public. The European Commission seeks to be more executive and active, because it has the means available to do so in its external relations. The budget for the EU's external relations is disproportionate to the means, actions and ends of its intra-regional budget.

This divergence in resource availability for internal and external affairs made a European Commission official wonder why there were not more grant proposals by third countries. He pointed out that there were significant leftover amounts for development cooperation (interview with European Commission official, 15 February 2009).

The IfS approximates the security and development spheres. It lowers the normative thresholds for international engagement. In particular, this is the case in instances when IfS is launched against the backdrop of exceptional circumstances of crises requiring immediate action. In 2009, the European Commission's annual report on IfS stated that Myanmar had been granted support for the purpose of conflict resolution and reconciliation, on top of the IfS support aimed at the post-Nargis recovery (European Commission 2010: 4). The decision of the European Commission was to adopt an Exceptional Assistance Measure under the IfS to support civil society in Myanmar in the run-up to the 2010 elections. It is debatable whether this type of support channelled through non-state actors undermines the official EU position. This discussion touches on the normative implications stemming from a securitised NTS perspective, which can override core norms and values of an actor and suggests that we should consider the EU as a normative actor on a case-by-case basis. The EU may compromise initial normative standards to launch the IfS, however, this could allow normative influence in the long run.

Summary of the EU as an actor

In the beginning of this book, we asked whether transboundary crises facilitate greater European engagement and recognition of the EU as an actor. We questioned whether European humanitarian, development and peace-keeping support can improve the EU's profile as a regional and collective politico-security actor in Southeast Asia. We also considered that post-Cold War European assistance efforts are shaped increasingly by an ethical understanding of security. This security perspective focuses on the reduction of risk for the welfare of states and their people. We further stated that in light of this, the NTS concept may therefore be considered as a stratagem.

By broadening the scope of what we understand as security, we imply a normative, namely liberal-democratic agenda through best-practice-sharing and other general risk reductive measures. This suggests the tacit continuation of the hierarchical relationship between ASEAN and the EU. It further highlights the importance of the question of the EU's normativity in its actions as well as the extent to which there are notions of threat 'othering' and convergence involved. Finally, the aspect of normative behaviour also touches upon the third guiding research question related to norm projection through inter-regionalism and the value of inter-regionalism in connection to crises in the ephemeral dynamics of the ASEAN-EU relationship.

The remainder of this chapter addresses these guiding research interests, raised at the beginning of this book. It determines the constraints of the EU as an actor on the basis of the discussed NTS challenges, which showed how crises or challenges facilitated greater interaction within and outside the regular frameworks of dialogue, and how they functioned as shapers of EU and ASEAN behaviour. The case studies demonstrated the extent to which the EU acted as a contemporary politico-security actor and suggested that the NTS perspective is increasingly providing a framework for engagement. This appears even more so in light of the eurozone crisis.

Domestic intra-European crises can act as potential triggers for action. In instances of domestic European crises, where the dependency pattern between the EU and Asia is reversed and the dependency level raised, cost-benefit calculations seem to kick in as the primary rationale behind European activism. The degree of affectedness and hence, the extent of threat construction appears of significant causality in explaining ASEAN–EU dynamics. Southeast Asia is far away. The NTS threat or crisis is generally neither immediate nor an actual threat to the EU, unless domestic circumstances compel European actors to re-consider and safeguard their own interests.

The case studies illustrated the EU as a multi-headed actor that drew upon an array of instruments to support ASEAN, including development and humanitarian assistance, CSDP, RRMs and other mechanisms to tackle the NTS challenges.[2] They displayed the various instruments of the EU's comprehensive toolkit in action and that the use of force is the EU's last resort. The use of force has not been applicable in the Southeast Asian context. The civilian arm of CSDP has been deployed in the case of the AMM; however, this was related to peace-keeping. The EU's broad understanding of security and its non-strategic or rather 'soft' approach to the region has seen the EU as a keen partner in the fields of disaster preparedness and crisis management.

The EU member states, European Commission, NGOs and state-affiliated organisations are the multiple heads that contribute to our understanding of the EU as a collective actor. EU engagement cuts across various European Commission DGs, the civilian arm of the CSDP, the bilateral interaction of the EU member states with ASEAN member states, ASEM, ASEAN–EU Ministerial Meetings and ARF. This book has shown that non-state actors are important actors involved in upholding EU identity and implementing EU projects. Implementing agencies have a significant on site presence and local knowledge. They are vital partners to the EU and the member states, if humanitarian aid has to be provided timely, effectively and remotely. The EU mainly acts as the liaison and donor body making available considerable financial support. Because in these instances, the EU rarely acts as the implementing body, it remains invisible and unidentifiable. The existing scholarly debate on the EU as a global actor has neglected the conceptualisation of the extent to which state-affiliated actors and NGOs have contributed to the EU's image and functionality as an actor. They are EU actors by proxy, which, on the one hand, enhance the EU's political profile, while, on the other, they de-emphasise the EU's supranational visibility.

The multiple heads of the EU can complicate a clear regional perspective on the EU as an actor. They blur the recognition by the sociological other. In the field of security, this recognition by the counterpart has become more complex since the establishment of CSDP. Until the creation of CSDP, Europe as a security actor has generally been associated with NATO and OSCE by the Southeast Asian side. Diverse intra-regional security perspectives and affiliations complicate a clear perception of the EU as a security actor. The only case that showed the EU as a clear-cut and significant collective politico-security actor in the aftermath of an NTS crisis was the case of the AMM. Specifically, the AMM provided evidence of the EU as an actor in reference to this book's definition of an NTS actor. The EU aggregated interests, formulated goals, made decisions and led the implementation of the mission. This is not to say that the European side did not aggregate interests and formulate goal, purposes and policies in response to the other NTS challenges.[3] However, the clarity of its agency was blurred by a variety of constraints. In the other cases, the EU was not a clear-cut actor. Its activities appeared indirect. There were also numerous other international actors who provided assistance and complicated a clear identification of the EU's assistance.

The EU's approach to Southeast Asia seeks to be minimally intrusive. Firstly, this is because of its foreign policy principle of a 'light footprint', which is compatible with the principle of non-interference. Here, one could also argue that the remoteness and secondary importance of Southeast Asia in the EU's politico-security calculations are favourable to 'light foot-print' engagement. Secondly, the Southeast Asian side has been persistent in keeping involvement of outside actors minimal and temporary. In some instances, the EU's commitment to non-interference has made the EU appear timid: in Chapter 5, an ASEAN Secretariat official was quoted to be unconvinced by the EU's normative agenda, because of its lenient stance on human rights, democracy and other values. By contrast, in the case of the Europa House in Aceh, the EU appeared to be pushing Indonesia's hospitality by extending the mandate and, thus, the boundaries of the principle of non-interference. These examples suggest that the EU as a norm-guided actor and projector of norms and values is highly variable.

In these case studies the variation of the EU and member states as normative actors depended on the degree of contagion and threat construction, the urgency to assist and the extent to which issues were addressed in the official dialogue mechanism. In times of crisis abroad and with the potential to harm the region, the EU acted according to the threat perceptions. The reaction to the AFC and avian influenza outbreak confirm this. Through the discussion of the trade and investment pledge, for instance, it was shown that the EU's response included a high degree of self-interest. Sometimes, the self-protective measures have been altruistically packaged. Crisis interpretations and threat constructions refer primarily to oneself.

In the case of the haze and political conflict in Aceh, EU interpretations of the Southeast Asian crises did not lead to apparent threat constructions. These crises were not immediate and did not trigger threat perceptions. However, the interpretation of these crises was still imperative for the EU to identify and justify EU assistance. The case of the political conflict in Aceh required substantive intra-European elite-to-elite persuasion to create an argument convincing enough for all member states to accept CSDP to be deployed to Aceh. There was no sudden surge of violence to convey urgency and support the persuasion process.

While the public was not directly involved in the decision-making process on the AMM, it was included indirectly when some member states opposed this mission on the grounds that such a deployment in a remote country did not benefit their electorates. Generally speaking, European crisis interpretations may be elitist, but they are sufficiently transparent and inclusive of public opinion. By contrast, Southeast Asian crisis-responsive learning processes are state-centric and elitist-driven. Considering this, many European projects in Southeast Asia aim to remedy the lack of this people-dimension. This focus on facilitating a greater people-dimension within Southeast Asian countries falls within the normative or liberal-democratic characteristic of the EU as an international actor.

The case of the Bali Bombings premised lower interdependence. Nevertheless, the EU was quick to condemn the attacks and launch the RRM. This demonstrated an instance where the EU's responsive action was based solely on the urgency triggered by the events. Here, the EU's normative identity was compromised to some extent, since Indonesia's human rights record was not an obstacle for the European Commission when launching the RRM. The EU has been demand-oriented in regard to this short-term and responsive action, focusing on providing a quick relief to the ill. At the same time, this book acknowledges that sometimes immediate normative goals are put into perspective to foster long-term normative goals.

Although the EU was unaffected in many of the discussed case studies, the chapters showed European solidarity and assistance to alleviate the severe plight of the affected populations. In such cases, the EU's supranational bodies and member states provided immediate assistance aiming at emergency relief. This has occasionally led to enhanced intra-regional, as well as inter-regional, cooperation. Many of these actions were identity-guided and not subject to lengthy political deliberations, as the introductory section on the Boxing Day Tsunami displayed. In particular, in instances of high interdependence, normative behaviour frequently paralleled cost-benefit calculations in developing a strategy to safeguard Europe.

As a general rule, if the overall rhetoric of the EU in relation to these NTS challenges displayed the EU's liberal-democratic agenda, there may be a case for describing the EU as a normative actor in terms of input. At the same time, the normative agenda may also serve as a frame for realising material interests. In particular, the NTS rhetoric building on common challenges and active solidarity tends to raise questions about the normative sincerity of the EU. Furthermore, when norms and values are compromised for the sake of dialogue and effectiveness, the output dimension appears generally consistent with interest-oriented actions; although there may be implicit long-term normative goals involved.

The following citation from a speech by Benita Ferrero-Waldner epitomises this ambiguity within the EU's behaviour,

> In our foreign policy we will prioritize conflict prevention and crisis management; promoting human rights and human security; and strengthening effective multilateralism. The EU firmly believes that preventing conflicts is not only a moral imperative, but also considerably less costly in the long run. We must address the root causes of conflicts and deny support to terrorism. We will continue to champion human rights and put particular emphasis on human security [and] respond to the full range of threats afflicting the most vulnerable in societies across the world, such as hunger, deadly diseases, environmental degradation and physical insecurity.
>
> (Ferrero-Waldner 2005)

This reflects the difficulty in disentangling the different logics behind the EU's actions. It exemplifies the behavioural tensions underpinning EU actions. That is, on the one hand, the EU's activities should be identity-consistent and based on a "moral imperative" (Ferrero-Waldner 2005). On the other hand, Ferrero-Waldner recognises that sometimes actions need to be pursued to avoid issues becoming "considerably less costly in the long run" (Ferrero-Waldner 2005). This mixed picture complicates the clear categorisation of the EU as a normative actor. Focusing on the output of EU actions provides only limited insights into the EU as a normative actor. In general, it is difficult to gauge whether the internalisation of norms took place or whether the Southeast Asian side was paying lip-service.

It appears that in instances of low interdependence and minimal domestic pressures, the EU is less inclined to act. The international community currently lacks cohesive indicators of when intervention or assistance is appropriate. To not act according to what is appropriate in the international community does not mean that the EU is not a normative actor. It appears that this is based on what the self deems appropriate in the first place.

Finally, the EU as a normative actor also relates to the method of norm projection. The transfer of norms through the inter-regional approach is a method that the EU has mastered. This takes into account that the inter-regional method has normative repercussions. Primarily, this is assumed because the method is based on regional integrative experiences that involve and generate specific norms and values. In the Introduction, it was argued that sharing the inter-regional experiences constitutes a method that shows the EU as a unique normative actor. Namely, this implies the transfer of norms including multilateralism, consensus, subsidiarity, permeable national sovereignty and others. These norms are salient to the inter-regional approach by the EU.

While it has been argued elsewhere that ASEAN has actively emulated EU institutions (Jetschke 2009), the case studies have shown that the European side is also very keen to share its regional experience with Southeast Asia. This may shape Southeast Asian regional integration according to the European model, buffering EU international legitimacy and influence. However, the case studies illustrated that the inter-regional level appears to be one of many EU foreign policies. In fact, many case studies displayed the significance of bilateral interactions. This is due to a variety of reasons that included, among others, the uneven degree of affectedness of ASEAN member states by the crisis, the institutional weakness of the ASEAN Secretariat and the prerogative of intergovernmental policies in some sectors. Although ASEAN–EU inter-regionalism relativises power asymmetries in comparison to bilateralism, recent world economic developments are more conducive to new bilateralism (Ravenhill 2003).

We cannot disassociate the trends in the economic realm from the political, since both realms are mutually reinforcing in terms of EU and EU member state power. In this sense, inter-regionalism is a complementary form of risk management to bilateralism. It is not an established and independent layer of global governance, but rather an occasional means of the EU to shape other regional settings; namely, contribute to economic growth and strengthen regional cohesion within the self and the counterpart. ASEAN–EU inter-regionalism has not been the prominent avenue of interaction and only contributes as one out of many sources to our understanding of the EU as a normative actor. It seems to be merely the seam between the national and global policy levels.

The following section moves beyond the query related to the lead questions. It specifically works out the prominent constraints of the EU as an actor/normative actor in cases of NTS crises in Southeast Asia. Firstly, domestic pressures – that is, for instance, the eurozone crisis or the example of the GAM leadership in exile in Sweden – can force national and regional authorities to act. Robert D. Putnam once argued that the concerns on the domestic level shape the international level (Putnam 1988).

Secondly, this book considers institutional variation and institutional governance costs on the regional and inter-regional level as significant constraints. The divergence in institutional history, structures and modes of interaction, in short, the asymmetry in institutional design,[4] may inhibit certain cooperative ambitions of the EU. Supranational and deep institutions provide a stronger basis for the enforcement of institutional standards and policies. The ASEAN Secretariat is softly institutionalised and mainly intergovernmentally steered by the member states. In comparison to the European Commission, the ASEAN Secretariat is under-staffed and -funded[5] to represent an appropriate dialogue and implementing partner.

Additionally, institutional inertia persists in many Southeast Asian states, despite liberalisation and democratisation processes. While NTS crises may stimulate normative change, Southeast Asia's institutional culture only shows minimal openness towards normative influence, even within the ASEAN Secretariat. The ASEAN Secretariat has the political will and ambition, but lacks the capacity and will of its member states to act.

Alongside the problem of resource shortage and institutional asymmetry, there is also the problem of the intergovernmental mode of cooperation. Overall, ASEAN member states prefer bilateral assistance and only show marginal interest in coordinating regional measures in cooperation with external partners (interview with Asian think tank representative, 10 November 2008). Since in Southeast Asia the states determine the implementation one-to-one, regional standards face enforcement problems, whether they are binding or not. Member states can even opt for defection, if the penalising function of the institution is weak.[6]

In Chapter 3, the rigid work ethics and hierarchical bureaucracies of some Asian states were portrayed as inhibitors to inter-regional interaction. Institutional norms associated with a specific institutional design influence the pace and nature of the inter-regional interaction. While this characteristic is inherent in institutions, it relates to the wider domestic reality. Beyond institutional problems which transpire from the national and regional levels, there are institutional issues located on the inter-regional and bilateral levels. An outdated Cooperation Agreement from 1980 and the current bilateral PCA negotiations excluding some member states do not necessarily support greater cohesion of the relationship.

The institutional design of inter-regional dialogue fora also constrains the EU as a normative actor by delimiting the practical and normative extent to which the EU and its member states can express their agenda. According to official ASEAN interviewees, in multilateral meetings, the Asian and European sides seemed to be more vocal about their normative stances. In particular, EU member states appeared more interest- and outcome-oriented in their bilateral discussions. They appeared less insistent on norms and values pertinent to the EU's identity (interview with ASEAN member state official, 2 November 2008).

In this context, it is insightful to refer to Kenneth A. Oye who has elucidated the difficulties with large numbers involved in actions. They raise questions of cost- and benefit-sharing and whether a collective action can be broken down into the sum of bilateral interactions (Oye 1986). Large numbers of members complicate bargaining processes and the EU as a whole mainly benefits in regard to its interests from the various bilateral interactions. Additionally, institutions confine an actor's normative behaviour through social pressure. If there is a large number of like-minded members that adhere to an institution's set of rules, they can exert social pressure on a member that defects. Although there are underlying institutionalised norms, social influence regularly trumps institutional norms.

Institutional costs from inter-regional interaction are contingent on an opportunity-cost balance. Regions will prioritise options of institutionalisation that involve low risk and low cost, mainly expressed through soft institutionalisation (Rüland 2002: 4–5). This minimises the risk of high costs when the benefits from the ASEAN–EU level are relatively low in comparison to their governance costs. The interaction between regional groupings enjoys a low level of confidence, and as a result it is expected that the ASEAN–EU level will remain focused on low-risk and low-cost approaches to institution-building. From this perspective, the ASEAN–EU level is set to remain a communicative channel aimed at sharing norms.

Another issue is the institutional overlap between the supranational and intergovernmental bodies, which complicates the effectiveness and representation of the EU as a collective actor. These grey areas have widened and are still in the process of extending, in particular, due to the continual broadening and deepening of international security concepts and the European Commission's increasing interest in proliferating its international actor profile. The EU is a fragmented and multi-headed political actor that depends on the supranational EU bodies as well as the national foreign ministers – in particular of the Big Three – and intergovernmental EU bodies. Regularly, the intergovernmental dimension of the EU's foreign policy has contributed to incoherent NTS policies.

On some NTS issues in Southeast Asia such as the case of avian influenza, the European Commission feels under-informed about the EU member states' bilateral activities. Despite the EU's intensive bureaucracy, there still seems to be a communication problem between the central organs of the EU and the member states. The internal competence overlap and communication and coordination problems within the EU have occasionally had a visible negative impact on the EU's image in Southeast Asia (interview with ASEAN member state official, 31 May 2010).

Defence and security are the prerogative of the EU member states. They are jealously guarded and require security projects that are carefully 'packaged' by the European Commission. For example, the European anti-terrorism agenda is dependent on national urgencies, threat perceptions and resources. Counter-terrorism activities are mainly defined nationally and carried out by the member states. For the European Commission to contribute towards counter-terrorism is a balancing act, demanding framing skills.

Finally, institutional similarity between two regions may also have a positive impact on the extent of convergence and inter-regional interaction. In light of future considerations of preparedness and tangible benefits, it is assumed that the EU will take a greater interest in interpreting and responding to crises where there are similar institutions and institutional contexts. This also applies to the aspect of geography. Geographic proximity necessitates dialogue and cooperation in the event of transnational NTS crises. Obviously, this does not apply to the ASEAN–EU relationship.

However, geographical distance is futile when there are significant functional dependencies between two regions far away from each. NTS crises occurring in regions of geographical and climatic similarity may attract EU interest, because they provide lessons to learn and offer an opportunity where adequate capabilities can be employed effectively. Since the discussed crises took place in the 'other' region and the European 'self' was, in most of the cases, not directly affected, the EU and its member states seemed to have been low-key in framing their engagement. Seemingly, when intra-regional crises and pressures rise, the EU begins to place stronger emphasis on rhetorical frames and the necessity to interact with Asia.

The final constraint defining the EU as an actor and normative actor relates to the systemic power distribution and the normative lining of the international realm. The environment of an actor influences the behaviour and the degree of normativity in its behaviour. This deviates from the reflectivist approach to some extent, since it views an actor's behaviour as constrained by exogenous norms and power realities. The transatlantic relationship and the USA–ASEAN relationship act as determinants of European engagement. However, the power asymmetry between and within the EU and ASEAN also sets the tone for the EU as an actor in the region. This asymmetry provides an unfavourable setting for cooperation on the same eye-level. Despite the common rhetoric of partnership and equality, the mindsets of the dialogue partners are still shaped by this asymmetry. Power asymmetries imply influence flows that may not be reciprocal

By means of the global communications advancement, Stephen D. Krasner has illustrated that asymmetric power distribution can subvert cooperation (Krasner 1991). The case studies could not verify this, but attested that the power asymmetries may contribute to the affirmation of the donor-recipient relationship. The NTS frame in the inter-regional context builds on the uneven socio-economic developments and Europe's advanced capabilities to assist. However, the cases have shown that power does not necessarily guarantee influence. The Southeast Asian side needs to be interested in the projects and actively involved in the implementation and internalisation. In the end, the ASEAN Secretariat and the Southeast Asian states determine the extent to which the activities are implemented. Power is relative to the situation and rather "the production, in and through social relations, of effects that shape the capacities of actors to determine their circumstances and fate" (Barnett and Duvall 2005: 42).

Even within the EU, power relations are to some extent social relations. This influences European interaction with Asia, as the case of the AMM exemplified. The EU as a normative actor is dependent on the ability of the member states to convince and compel other member states about their normative interests. Prior to the launch of the AMM, Solana and the Nordic states managed to persuade fellow CSDP states that it was a necessity to engage in Aceh on the basis of solidarity and moral responsibility. The Nordic states did not apply power capabilities, but based their argumentation on the feasibility and appropriateness of action.

Conclusions

This chapter addressed the research interests outlined in the beginning of this book. It discussed the central features of the EU as an actor and normative actor based on the empirical evidence. The case studies crystallised the nuances of the EU as a normative actor and affirmed that the NTS crises enhanced EU activism towards Southeast Asia. They recognised that the only foreign policy method with normative characteristics unique to the EU is inter-regionalism. However, inter-regionalism proved to be a less prominent path in the case studies. The NTS challenges further identified the EU as a multi-headed actor with a variety of short- and long-term instruments at its disposal. In particular, this discussion related to the level of interdependence, threat construction and urgency of assistance as the key determinants in gauging the extent of altruism and cost-benefit calculations driving EU actions. The normative liberal-democratic agenda underpinning EU actions directly or indirectly mainly defines the EU as a normative actor in terms of input. Overall, the output dimension of this agenda is difficult to detect, because of issues of lipservice, vagueness of measuring the micro-level impact and other circumstances.

The chapter acknowledged that NTS challenges promoted the continuous asymmetry in the ASEAN–EU relationship since they focused on the diverging socio-economic developments on the inter-regional level. It further discussed the four constraints vital in understanding the EU as an actor: domestic constraints, institutional design, geographical proximity and systemic power asymmetries. Seemingly, the EU as an actor in relation to NTS crises only mattered to ASEAN on a case-by-case basis and with particular regard to development and humanitarian assistance. Nevertheless, NTS provides an important and contemporary avenue of engagement. The EU understands its limitations as a latecomer in Southeast Asia. The NTS concept may assist the EU in finding a niche for itself as a valuable actor in the region.

Notes

1 Energy security concerns are pertinent to both developed and developing economies and provide an issue area of enhanced cooperation between the EU and ASEAN. At the same time, the EU recognises that future cooperation in this area has to be sensitive to food/agricultural, environmental, socio-economic and nuclear energy implications in Southeast Asia.
2 There are only individual member states which are actively pushing for a greater strategic role. For example, at the 11th Shangri-La Dialogue in 2012, the French Minister of Defence, Jean-Yves Le Drian, said that France is a power in the Asia-Pacific (please see the full speech at www.iiss.org/conferences/the-shangri-la-dialogue/shangri-la-dialogue-2012/speeches/?esctl3017559espagelisterespager_p=4,

accessed on 24 June 2012). In a time of austerity, it will be interesting to see whether in the near future the EU as a collective actor will change its operational capabilities and strategies to adapt to the ambition and rhetoric of individual states and pursue its pivot to Asia.

3 For example, the EU's general pattern of engagement on the described NTS crises included initial research endeavours, fact-finding missions or joint information exchange with Southeast Asia. These initial missions paved the way for collaborative efforts. Proposals are made in consultation with the Southeast Asian side, projects devised and financial resources made available on the basis of these initial fact-finding missions. This initial pattern of engagement was described in the case of the AMM, as well as in Chapter 5 in regard to the expert team that was sent to Southeast Asia in the aftermath of the Bali Bombings.

4 The book is based on a broad understanding of institutions comprising political organisations and policy bodies as well as normative standards.

5 Its budget is constituted by equal shares of its member states. This implies that the poorest state determines the scope of the budget. For example, for 2010, this budget was only US$14 million.

6 For example, despite an ASEAN Intergovernmental Commission on Human Rights, the interpretation of human rights is subject to the individual ASEAN member states' assessment. In some cases, there is a clear discrepancy between the international standards, terms of reference and the evaluation of member states. This is not to say that the EU supranational level is not regulatory and without reliance on the member states in terms of enforcement.

Conclusion

> In conclusion, in a world where we face multiple and continually evolving security threats, building strong partnerships between like-minded regions has never been more important. The EU is a true Asian partner – our interest is not in projecting power but in empowering. The EU's unique comprehensive approach also makes us a highly effective partner.
> (International Institute for Strategic Studies/Baroness Ashton 2013)

The case studies have shown that over the years the EU's security perspective towards Southeast Asia has sharpened. The EU has become increasingly aware of the risks stemming from interdependence and recognises that the dividing lines between national and international security have faded. The preceding chapters have adopted this security perspective and drawn upon an NTS frame to understand the EU as a contemporary actor in Southeast Asia. The NTS perspective showed that the EU's activism towards the region has increased. The chapters referred to the selected NTS crises as moments where norms could become unstable and where ASEAN was open to European assistance. These instances also acted as catalysts for enhanced European norm-sharing. NTS is a concept that underlines the construction of common threat perceptions and areas of cooperation that imply tacit forms of normative influence. The NTS concept builds on socio-economic developments and reflects the power asymmetry in the ASEAN–EU relationship, as well as the difference in the liberal-democratic agenda.

The discussion suggested that there were processes of politicisation involved in terms of threat 'othering'[1] and 'commonalisation'. The former implies an understanding that the EU is vulnerable in the global economy and that it needs to safeguard itself from the vulnerabilities and risks of others, even from those regions that are far away. The method of threat 'othering' correlates and builds on threat 'commonalisation'. In this context, the discussion of the case studies indicated that engagement in Southeast Asia was conducive to a cooperative and trade-favourable environment. Cost-benefit calculations are important and frequently underpin the EU's actions, while, at the same time, the EU's rhetoric of solidarity and normativity is drawn upon often.

In spite of the EU's official norm- and value-laden rhetoric, the case studies raised concerns about the EU's normative identity and underlined the tensions between the security and development spheres. The NTS frame does not entirely discount the concept of the EU as a normative actor in the ASEAN–EU relationship. However, the question of EU normativity has become blurred and can only be understood in a nuanced manner superseding traditional conceptualisations *à la* normative power by Ian Manners (2002).

To complement the topical debate on the EU as a normative actor in international affairs, this book has crystallised that the variability of the EU as a normative actor is contingent on the level of interdependence, substance of the existing relationship with the counterpart, severity of crisis and the relative power of the counterpart. On the operational level, one can generalise that the EU as a normative actor is expressed through the reaction to the NTS crisis; the preference for the responsive tool and implementing actor; the variation in direct or indirect and long-term or short-term focus; and the integration of norms and values into the operation. The latter aspect by itself already allows a basic definition of the EU as a self-proclaimed normative actor on the basis of the normative input level. However, such a basic definition should be scrutinised and extended to incorporate the output level of EU actions. This would take into account the extent to which the EU can diffuse and see its norms and values adopted, or even internalised.

In the past, the EU has played on its norms and values – more or less successfully – to assume a distinct international profile. The contemporary eurozone crisis implies more toned down normative demands in the EU's external relations. It places greater emphasis on the NTS frame as an avenue for advancing effective cooperation and indirect normative influence with Southeast Asia. The NTS frame is helpful in discerning normative and rationalist behaviour. However, as previously alluded to, its origins render it a crude and highly sensitised concept that challenges the normative dimension of an international actor. The chapters have shown that the EU is a flexible normative actor that manages to uphold its normative identity and be inclusive of non-state actors. NTS emphasises the importance of national and regional authorities in managing risk, but, at the same time, it does not necessarily shift the focus away from participatory elements. In fact, it can assist in promoting non-hegemonic notions of security that entail the everyday security of the individual in society becoming more important. This interpretation of NTS strengthens the understanding of the EU as a multilateral and soft-power-based actor and supports comprehensive forms of resilience among the small powers of Southeast Asia. Such a conception of NTS can act as a facilitator frame for greater EU politico-security influence through both the regional and state level.

In the beginning, I articulated three research questions that acted as leads for the empirical discussion. The preceding chapter and the previous paragraphs summed up further central insights on the question of normativity. The following paragraphs will summarise the central responses to the question: *Can the EU, a remote power, improve its profile as a collective (politico-security) actor through humanitarian and peace-keeping support in a region pre-occupied with strategic concerns?*

Premising the EU as an actor in relation to NTS crises implies the recognition that the EU is either an NTS actor or an actor on NTS challenges, as defined in Chapter 1. The utility of the NTS frame as an avenue to gauge the EU as an NTS actor or actor on NTS issues is contentious, since humanitarian and development assistance in the case studies were not necessarily considered along security lines by the EU and the Southeast Asian governments and publics. In the case studies, the EU and its member states acted predominantly as development assistance providers. NTS had only limited applicability as a distinctive way of framing the EU as an actor. While the NTS frame enhanced EU interaction, it remains to be seen whether it can upgrade the politico-security profile of the EU causally.

The 2000s have seen greater recognition of the security-development nexus by the EU and an expansion of security encroaching upon the development sphere. However, the concept of NTS itself did not receive systematic attention by the EU. In 2003, the ASEAN–EU Ministerial Meeting took brief note of this concept. Issue-specific cooperation enhanced and deepened but did not see an explicit entrenchment of the NTS concept within the official ASEAN–EU rhetoric until many years later, at the ASEM Foreign Ministers' Meeting Working Together on Non-traditional Security Challenges on 7 June 2011 in Gödöllő, Hungary (Maier-Knapp 2011a). Until then, the EU has pursued only an implicit approach on NTS within the ASEAN–EU relationship. Today, the NTS approach is explicit within this relationship and pertains to contemporary international risk-preventive dynamics.

There were some cases that revealed that the EU's intentions were based on security calculations. In these instances, the EU and its member states targeted the NTS threat directly, as well as indirectly. Indirect actions based on threat perceptions pinpoint the EU as an NTS actor. For example, in Chapter 4, the European Commission's perception of international terrorism mismatched its competency. Direct actions were congruent to threat perceptions and, therefore, in this case, one could describe the EU as an NTS actor. By contrast, in instances where Southeast Asia identified an NTS threat, but where the EU responded with development and humanitarian instruments, and outlined objectives unrelated to the Southeast Asian insecurity, the EU was not an NTS actor. Since it did not adopt a security lens on these issues, it rather acted as an actor on NTS issues. The utility of the NTS frame is circumstantial and subjective. First and foremost, it is a stratagem for engagement and best-practice-sharing, when considered from a European perspective. From a Southeast Asian perspective, it is a stratagem for extracting financial and technical support from the EU. The majority of Southeast Asian countries rely on external cooperation to drive development and integrate into the global economy.

Overall, the book has shown that the EU has contributed to the increased level of preparedness and mitigated the vulnerability of the ASEAN states in specific sectors. However, in Southeast Asia's security environment, it does not suffice to be an economic power or the champion of development assistance. Military muscle is important and impacts the perception and role expectations of the ASEAN states. While NTS may act as a stepping stone towards a more coherent, influential and robust EU collective politico-security profile in Southeast Asia, it is only one avenue for engagement, which is open to many other actors. Nevertheless, NTS challenges will shape the future of the EU as a contemporary actor with and within Southeast Asia. Both sides will continue promoting multi-level and cross-sectoral day-to-day, risk-pre-emptive and crisis-responsive activities. The EU will pre-select and concentrate on deeper cooperation in niche areas and provide selective engagement where it believes to be able to provide additional value and have a comparative advantage. In light of the non-hegemonic, issue-specific and multilateralist quality inherent in the NTS approach, multilateral dialogue fora will receive continuous support.

So, what does this imply for the final lead question regarding the ASEAN–EU dialogue: *What is the value of the existing ASEAN–EU dialogue as an institution for inter-regional cooperation? If crises function as stimulus for enhanced interaction within the ASEAN–EU relationship, does this indicate that the existing dialogue does not carry sufficient weight to further inter-regional communication and coordination?* Through the European NTS lens, ASEAN will continue to be an important region of concern and the reference point for the development of joint activities. This facilitates active inter-regional experience-sharing, strengthening regional cohesion in Southeast Asia and proliferating the EU's political role. The nation-state as a whole will continue to be considered as the

NTS referent from the European perspective. This rivals conventional Asian treatments of the NTS concept that exclude the people-dimension and de-emphasise a greater inter-regional focus.

The EU as an international actor in regions far from Europe

Based on the previous discussions, we can conclude that geography is no longer a given reality. In fact, one can argue that Singapore may be closer to the EU in geo-economic terms than some countries at the periphery of the EU. The interdependence of the global economy appears to be the dominant narrative redefining the proximity of international actors. With this comes a new understanding of risk and insecurity that includes the active threat 'othering' and 'commonalisation' of other regions. In light of this, NTS poses a suitable frame of engagement and analysis. At the same time, it needs to be re-engineered to suit the ASEAN–EU interaction and set itself apart from the traditional developmental and humanitarian approach of the EU to Southeast Asia.

The EU is an alternative security actor in the region. It has the capabilities and mediation expertise to be of value. It possesses the financial resources and multiple actors to develop and sustain partnerships with the region. ASEAN does find the EU to be an appealing partner on peacekeeping and disaster relief, in spite of its geographical distance. In fact, it may be this geographical distance as well as the lack of strategic calculations and presence which make the EU an attractive alternative partner to countries caught up in the great power rivalry.

In a way, the NTS frame heralds in the EU as a different type of EU as international actor. It premises that every international actor knows by now that the EU has a liberal-democratic and multilateralist identity, which it will attempt to project in its external relations. In this light, the NTS frame downplays the securitisation of development cooperation and the illiberal implications of the development-security nexus. It presumes that the counterparts are aware of this and that they understand that this underlies practice-oriented cooperation with the EU. Implicitly, this perspective renders conceptions of normative power EU obsolescent. In the end, the conundrum rests with the EU itself: and with the critics of the idea of the EU as a normative power who have to come to terms with the fact that the degree of normativity expressed in the EU's external relations is not nullified by the NTS frame and could strengthen the EU's normative profile in the long run. This is the case, because the NTS perspective accounts for an international strategy that is typical to non-hegemonic and multilateralist actors in world affairs.

NTS also provides an interesting opportunity for the EU to foster intraregional coherence in the context of the European External Action Service

(EEAS).² The NTS lens towards Southeast Asia holds the potential to enhance the EEAS internal coordination, because it allows the streamlining of the operational mode among the various stakeholders involved in producing the EU's external policy. It may mitigate competence overlaps through a specification of the various NTS threats. One could argue that a securitised perspective avoids lengthy decision-making processes. Then again, this may counter the EU's normative identity. In the worst case, it may only veneer the underlying institutional tension between the European Commission and the EU member states by providing a frame to better align national and EU external policies. It may ease the supranational versus national dichotomy, while entrenching the disconnect between the national and European identities as international actors. As this book has premised, if ideas and identity are shapers of behaviour, they need to be sufficiently attuned to the EU as an overall actor. Thus, it will be interesting to see whether the NTS frame can act as a hinge or ends up as a wedge between the EU's multiple heads.

Conclusively, this book has shown, firstly, that NTS crises enhanced EU activism towards Southeast Asia. Secondly, it has outlined that the NTS perspective has contributed to the EU's politico-security and normative profile to some extent. This has been mainly in an implicit sense that emphasises the EU's ability to share regional best practices. If practices are always embedded in a specific cultural context, does the EU then have to continue telling others who it is and how these actors ought to behave? Arguably, in light of the EU's well-known and self-proclaimed normative profile in world affairs, one could say that this toned down normative influence suffices. Of course, this is not without controversies and, indeed, the restatement of one's own normative identity is important, as political leaders and bureaucracies come and go, and people do forget.

Construing broader implications

In the beginning, it was said that the EU likes to claim itself to be complementary to the American security engagement in the region. In theory, the NTS frame serves this purpose, as it creates a narrative that is based on a broad, non-hegemonic and dialogue-oriented definition of common security. Understanding the EU as a normative and politico-security actor, which can contribute to the stability and cohesion of Southeast Asia pertains to the grand debates of international relations theorising. This is because in an international structure of complex interdependence, we cannot rely on the American hard power and hegemonic approach to the Southeast Asian region.

In a world of multilateralisms, transnational networks and other forms of multi-level and multi-actor cooperation, we cannot merely focus on the regional powers. We cannot exclusively rely on materialist and rationalist treatments of the international relations of the Asia-Pacific. Die-hard realists need to acknowledge that security is also about instilling cooperative behaviour. It should be about socialisation and dialogue on common security challenges. A stable and secure Asia-Pacific necessitates the active inclusion of China into the security architecture. This implies the strengthening and socialisation of China's neighbours, whether they are middle, small powers or no powers.

The crisis in Europe is compelling greater European outward orientation and providing the momentum for a greater NTS dialogue with the Asia-Pacific. In light of this, it is time to revisit the EU as an actor in Southeast Asia and think about the potential theoretical and practical benefits of functionalist theorising and the common security concept – coined by the EU. In a time of an irrational North Korean leader and an assertive rising power, it could be interesting to explore contemporary dynamics in the Asia-Pacific along non-hegemonic and humanist lines.

Notes

1 In particular, Myanmar until recently has been the EU's prominent target and object of threat 'othering', as mentioned in Chapter 1. In relation to human rights and NTS threats, Myanmar was referred to as the destabilising element within the ASEAN region. Undoubtedly, a variety of NTS threats ranging from drug trafficking to infectious diseases stem from Myanmar. However, the EU's emphasis on Myanmar distorts the fact that there are other ASEAN member states which are also of concern to their neighbours, as according to this book in the case of the haze, where Indonesia thwarted regional integrative dynamics.
2 EEAS was created to support the High Representative for Foreign Affairs and Security Policy. Its creation suggests that the EU is working to become a more coherent and recognisable international actor. By emulating to some extent the state in its structure and work mode of the diplomatic and foreign services, the EEAS may stimulate greater recognition of the EU as an actor. Theoretically, EEAS has the structural capacity to overcome the gap between recognition by the sociological 'other' and the actions of the EU. First and foremost, the EEAS should be seen as the outward-oriented extension of the EU's advanced internal integration process. It is a reinvention of the supranational dimension to strengthen the European position in the world.

Bibliography

Aceh Monitoring Mission (2005). Aceh Monitoring Mission (Retrieved 19.04.2008, from www.aceh-mm.org/).
Acharya, A. (2004). How Ideas Spread: Whose Norms Matter? Norm Localization and Institutional Change in Asian Regionalism. *International Organization*, 58(Spring), pp. 239–275.
Acharya, A., M. Caballero Anthony and R. Emmers (eds.) (2006). *Non-Traditional Security in Asia: Dilemmas in Securitisation*. Aldershot: Ashgate.
Aggestam, L. (2006). Role Theory and European Foreign Policy: A Framework of Analysis. In O. Elgström and M. Smith (eds.), *The European Union's Role in International Politics*. London: Routledge, pp. 11–26.
Aggestam, L. (2008). Introduction: Ethical Power Europe? *International Affairs*, 84(1), pp. 1–11.
Agence France Press (19 March 2004). WHO Warns Vietnam about Bird Flu, ProMED-mail (Retrieved 15.11.2010, from www.promedmail.org/pls/apex/f?p=2400:1202:3818374213884994::NO::F2400_P1202_CHECK_DISPLAY,F2400_P1202_PUB_MAIL_ID:X,24787).
Agence France Press (22 January 2004). Suspected Outbreak of Fowl Cholera in Laos, Borneo Bulletin (Retrieved 15.11.2010, from www.brunei-online.com/bb/thu/jan22w10.htm).
Agence France Press (23 April 2008). EU Mulls New Myanmar Sanctions, as Constitution Vote Closes In (Retrieved 15.11.2010, from www.euro-burma.eu/doc/April2008.pdf).
Allen, D. and M. Smith (1991). Western Europe's Presence in the Contemporary International Arena. In M. Holland (ed.), *The Future of European Political Cooperation*. New York: St. Martin's Press, pp. 95–120.
Allen, D. and M. Smith (1998). The European Union's Security Presence: Barrier, Facilitator, or Manager. In C. Rhodes (ed.), *The European Union in the World Community*. London: Lynne Rienner, pp. 45–63.
ARF (2009). ASEAN Regional Forum List of Track I Activities Year 1994–2009 (Retrieved 02.02.2010, from www.aseanregionalforum.org/PublicLibrary/ARFActivities/ListofARFTrackIActivitiesBySubject/tabid/94/Default.aspx).

ARF member states (1998). *Chairman's Statement* presented at the Fifth Meeting of the ASEAN Regional Forum (Retrieved 30.09.2009, from www.aseanregionalforum.org/PublicLibrary/RFChairmansStatementsandReports/ChairmansStatementofthe5thMeetingoftheASE/tabid/180/Default.aspx).

ASEAN and Asian Development Bank researchers (2001). *Fire, Smoke and Haze: the ASEAN Response Strategy*. Jakarta: Asian Development Bank.

ASEAN and EU member states (2000). *Vientiane Declaration of the 13th ASEAN–EU Ministerial Meeting* presented at the 13th ASEAN–EU Ministerial Meeting (Retrieved 30.09.2009, from www.aseansec.org/5644.htm).

ASEAN and EU member states (27–28 January 2003). *Joint Co-Chairman's Statement* presented at the 14th ASEAN–EU Ministerial Meeting in Brussels (Retrieved 12.11.2008, from www.asean.org/news/item/14th-eu-asean-ministerial-meeting-brussels-27-28-january-2003).

ASEAN and EU member states (2005). *Joint Co-Chairmen's Statement of the 15th ASEAN–EU Ministerial Meeting* presented at the ASEAN–EU Ministerial Meeting (Retrieved 21.12.2009, from www.aseansec.org/17354.htm).

ASEAN and EU member states (2007). *Plan of Action to Implement the Nuremberg Declaration on an EU–ASEAN Enhanced Partnership* (Retrieved 12.11.2008, from www.aseansec.org/21122.pdf).

ASEAN and EU member states (26–27 April 2012). *Co-Chairs' Statement of the 19th ASEAN–EU Ministerial Meeting* (Retrieved 09.01.2011, from www.consilium.europa.eu/uedocs/cms_data/docs/pressdata/EN/foraff/129883.pdf).

ASEAN and EC member states (1974). *Joint Statement* presented at the Informal Meeting of ASEAN Ministers and Vice-President and Commissioner of the European Commission (Retrieved 30.06.2009, from www.aseansec.org/5615.htm).

ASEAN and EC member states (1978). *Joint Declaration* presented at the ASEAN–EC Ministerial Meeting (Retrieved 12.04.2008, from www.aseansec.org/5617.htm).

ASEAN and EC member states (1980). *Joint Statement on Political Issues* (Retrieved 30.06.2009, from www.aseansec.org/5622.htm).

ASEAN and EC member states (1983). *Joint Declaration of the 4th AEMM* (Retrieved 30.06.2009, from www.aseansec.org/5628.htm).

ASEAN and EC member states (1988). *Joint Declaration of the 7th AEMM* (Retrieved 30.06.2009, from www.aseansec.org/5636.htm).

ASEAN and EC member states (1991). *Joint Declaration of the 9th AEMM* (Retrieved 30.06.2009, from www.aseansec.org/5638.htm).

ASEAN Ministers on the Environment (2006). *Joint Press Statement* presented at the 10th ASEAN Ministerial Meeting on the Environment (Retrieved 30.06.2009, from www.aseansec.org/18917.htm).

ASEAN member states and European Commission (1999). *Joint Press Release* presented at the 13th ASEAN–European Commission Joint Cooperation Committee Meeting (Retrieved 30.09.2009, from www.aseansec.org/5653.htm).

ASEAN member states (2005). *Co-chairs' Summary Report of the ARF Workshop on Civil Military Operations* (Retrieved 12.06.2009, from www.aseanregionalforum.org/PublicLibrary/ARFChairmansStatementsandReports/tabid/66/Default.aspx).

ASEM Finance Ministers (1997). *Chairman's Statement* presented at the First Asia–Europe Finance Ministers' Meeting (Retrieved 21.10.2009, from www.ec.europa.eu/external_relations/asem/meetings/finmin_1_en.pdf).

ASEM Finance Ministers (1999). *Chairman's Statement* presented at the Second ASEM Foreign Ministers' Meeting (Retrieved 21.10.2009, from www.ec.europa.eu/external_relations/asem/meetings/finmin_2_en.pdf).

ASEM member states (1998). *Chairman's Statement of the Second Asia–Europe Meeting* (Retrieved 13.07.2009, from www.aseminfoboard.org/content/documents/chairmans_statement_asem_2.pdf).

Associated Press (11 November 2005). China Reports New Bird-Flu Outbreaks, CTV (Retrieved 22.04.2010, from www.calgary.ctv.ca/servlet/an/local/CTVNews/20051111/bird_flu_china_051111?hub=MontrealHome).

Australian Federal Police (2008). Bali Bombings 2002 (Retrieved 12.05.2010, from www.afp.gov.au/international/operations/previous_operations/bali_bombings_2002.html).

Auvinen, J. and R. Wright (2009). What ambitions for the civilian ESDP? In Á. de Vasconcelos (ed.), *What ambitions for European defence in 2020?* Paris: EUISS, pp. 111–122.

Axelrod, R. and R.O. Keohane (1986). Achieving Cooperation under Anarchy: Strategies and Institutions. In K. A. Oye (ed.), *Cooperation under Anarchy*. Princeton: Princeton University Press, pp. 226–254.

Barnett, M. and R. Duvall (2005). Power in International Politics. *International Organization*, 59(1), pp. 39–75.

Berkofsky, A. (2003). Can the EU Play a Meaningful Role in Asian Security through the ASEAN Regional Forum? *EIAS Policy Brief*, 3(1).

Biscop, S. (2008). *Permanent Structured Cooperation and the Future of ESDP*. Brussels: Egmont – The Royal Institute for International Relations.

Blustein, P. and K. Richburg (16 June 1998). Fears about Asia hit World Stocks. *Washington Post* (Retrieved 16.07.2009, from www.washingtonpost.com/wp-srv/business/longterm/asiaecon/stories/asia061698.htm).

Boisseau du Rocher, S. (2012). The European Union, Burma/Myanmar and ASEAN: a Challenge to European Norms and Values or a New Opportunity? *Asia Europe Journal*, 10(2/3) pp. 165–180.

Booth, S. and S. Herbert (2011). *EU External Aid: Who Is It For?* London: Open Europe.

Braud, P. -A. and G. Grevi (2005). The EU mission in Aceh: implementing peace. *Occasional Paper* (61).

Bretherton, C. and J. Vogler (eds.) (2006). *The European Union as a Global Actor*. New York: Routledge.

Bridges, B. (1999). Europe and the Asian Financial Crisis: coping with contagion. *Asian Survey*, 39(3), pp. 456–467.

Brittan, S. L. (1999). Europe/Asia relations. *The Pacific Review*, 12(3), pp. 491–498.
Brooke, S. and R. S. Leiken (2005). Al Qaeda's Second Front: Europe. *The New York Times* (Retrieved 24.01.2010, from www.nytimes.com/2005/07/14/opinion/14iht-edleiken.html).
Bünte, M. and C. Portela (2012). Myanmar: the Beginning of Reforms and the End of Sanctions. *GIGA Focus* (3).
Buzan, B., O. Waever and J. de Wilde (1998). *Security: a new framework for analysis*. London: Lynne-Rienner.
Chalermpalanupap, T. (2010). ASEAN's Policy of Enhanced Interactions. In A. Rieffel (ed.), *Myanmar/Burma: inside challenges, outside interests*. Washington DC: Brookings Institution Press, pp. 150–165.
Caballero Anthony, M. (2009). Challenging Change: Nontraditional Security, Democracy, and Regionalism. In D. K. Emmerson (ed.), *Hard Choices: Security, Democracy, and Regionalism in Southeast Asia*. Stanford: Walter H. Shorenstein Asia-Pacific Research Centre, pp. 191–217.
Cook, A. (2010). Positions of Responsibility: a comparison of ASEAN and EU approaches towards Myanmar, *International Politics*, 47(3/4), pp. 433–449.
Council for Asia–Europe Cooperation (2000). *Asia–Europe Cooperation: Beyond the Financial Crisis*. Singapore: Institute of Southeast Asian Studies.
Council of the European Union (2001). *Council Regulation (EC) No 381/2001 of 26 February 2001 creating a rapid-reaction mechanism* (Retrieved 13.05.2009, from www.europa.eu/eur-lex/pri/en/oj/dat/2001/l_057/l_05720010227en00050009.pdf).
Council of the European Union (2003). European Security Strategy: a Secure Europe in a Better World (Retrieved 19.11.2005, from www.ue.eu.int/uedocs/cmsUpload/78367.pdf).
Council of the European Union (2006a). Council Joint Action on the European Union Monitoring Mission in Aceh (Indonesia). *Chaillot Paper*, VI(87).
Council of the European Union (2006b). *Regulation (EC) No 1717/2006 of the European Parliament and of the Council of 15 November 2006 establishing an Instrument for Stability* (Retrieved 26.05.2009, from www.eur-lex.europa.eu/LexUriServ/site/en/oj/2006/l_327/l_32720061124en00010011.pdf).
Council of the European Union (2007). *COASI advice on the Aceh Monitoring Mission (AMM), including lessons learned about EU-ASEAN cooperation in the light of this experience*. Brussels: European Commission.
Croissant, A. and N. Schwank (2006). Violence, Extremism and Transformation: Bertelsmann Transformation Index 2006 Findings. In Bertelsmann Foundation (ed.), *Violence, Extremism and Transformation*. Gütersloh: Bertelsmann Stiftung.
Delegation of the European Commission to Indonesia and Brunei Darussalam. *Beyond the Tsunami: From Recovery to Peace* (Retrieved 26.03.09, from www.delidn.ec.europa.eu/en/special/tsunami.htm).
Dennis, R. (1998). EU-Forest Fire Prevention and Control Project (Retrieved 10.03.2010, from www.fire.uni-freiburg.de/se_asia/projects/eu.html).

Bibliography

Dennis, R. (1999). *A Review of Fire Projects in Indonesia (1982–1998)*. Bogor: Center for International Forestry Research.

Deputy Prime Minister of Cambodia (2009). Keynote Address at the 17th ASEAN–EU Ministerial Meeting, CNV Team (Retrieved 06.10.2009, from www.cnv.org.kh).

Dosch, J. (2003). Changing Security Cultures in Europe and Southeast Asia: implications for inter-regionalism. *Asia Europe Journal*, 1(4), pp. 483–501.

Dosch, J. (2008). ASEAN's Reluctant Liberal Turn and the Thorny Road to Democracy Promotion. *The Pacific Review*, 21(4), pp. 527–545.

Dosch, J., L. MacKellar, D. van Esbroeck and M. Coenegrachts (2011). *Evaluation of the European Commission's Cooperation with the Philippines*. Freiburg: Particip.

Duchêne, F. (1972). Europe's Role in World Peace. In R. J. Mayne (ed.), *Europe Tomorrow: Sixteen Europeans Look Ahead*. London: Fontana, pp. 32–47.

Emmers, R. (2004). *Non-Traditional Security in the Asia-Pacific: The Dynamics of Securitisation*. Singapore: Marshall Cavendish.

EU Delegation to Indonesia and Brunei Darussalam (2009). Beyond the Tsunami: From Recovery to Peace (Retrieved 21.10.2009, from www.delidn.ec.europa.eu/en/special/tsunami.htm).

EU High Representative Javier Solana (2003). *European Security Strategy* (Retrieved 15.07.2008, from www.consilium.europa.eu/uedocs/cmsUpload/78367.pdf).

European Commission (1998). EU Support to Help Tackle Asian Financial Crisis: European Network of Financial Experts to Be Established. *Single Market News* (Retrieved 13.10.2009 from www.ec.europa.eu/internal_market/smn/smn14/s14mn08.htm).

European Commission (2002). *Indonesia – European Commission Strategy Paper 2002–2006* (Retrieved 05.11.2008, from www.ec.europa.eu/external_relations/indonesia/csp/02_06_en.pdf).

European Commission (2003). *A New Partnership with South East Asia* (Retrieved 12.11.2008, from www.eurosoutheastasia-ict.org/docs/anewpartnership.pdf).

European Commission (2004). *Regional Indicative Programme 2005–2006 ASEAN* (Retrieved 04.11.2008, from www.ec.europa.eu/external_relations/asean/csp/rip_05-06_en.pdf).

European Commission (2006). *Indonesia – European Commission Strategy Paper 2007–2013* (Retrieved 04.11.2009, from www.ec.europa.eu/europeaid/where/asia/documents/indonesia_csp_2007-2013_en.pdf).

European Commission (2009). *Forging Closer Co-operation with South East Asia* (Retrieved 04.11.2009, from www.ec.europa.eu/europeaid/where/asia/regional-cooperation/support-regional-integration/asean_en.htm).

European Commission (2010). *2009 Annual Report from the European Commission on the Instrument for Stability*. Brussels: European Commission.

European Commission (28 September 2010). *Report from the Comission to the European Parliament, the Council, the European Economic and Social Committee and the Committee of the Regions: 2009 Annual Report from the European Commission on the Instrument for Stability*. Brussels: European Commission.

European Commission Humanitarian Aid Office (2007). *Disaster Preparedness: Regional Initiatives in Southeast Asia* (Retrieved 21.10.2008, from www.ec.europa.eu/echo/files/policies/dipecho/presentations/se_asia_11_07_en.pdf).

European Council (1992). *Treaty on European Union* (Retrieved 13.12.2005, from www.europa.eu.int/en/record/mt/heads.html).

European Council (1999). *Declaration of the European Council on strengthening the common European Policy on Security and Defence* (Retrieved 14.11.2005, from www.basicint.org/europe/ESDP/0699-PR_EUdefpol.htm).

European Council (2002). *Council Conclusions on the Terrorist Attacks in Bali, Indonesia*. Brussels: European Council.

European Council (2008). *Report on the Implementation of the European Security Strategy: Providing Security in a Changing World* (Retrieved 13.01.2009, from www.consilium.europa.eu/ueDocs/cms_Data/docs/pressdata/EN/reports/104630.pdf).

European Council President (8 November 2011). *Combating Malnutrition through Sustainable Interventions: EU–ASEAN Relations as Key Driver*, speech by Herman Van Rompuy President of the European Council at the AECA Conference (Retrieved 18.02.2012, from www.consilium.europa.eu/uedocs/cms_data/docs/pressdata/en/ec/125961.pdf).

EU member states (2007). *Treaty of Lisbon* (Retrieved 12.04.2009, from www.bookshop.europa.eu/eubookshop/download.action?fileName=FXAC07306ENC_002.pdf&eubphfUid=534817&catalogNbr=FX-AC-07-306-EN-C).

Evans, P. (2004). Human Security and East Asia: In the Beginning. *Journal of East Asian Studies*, 4, pp. 263–284.

Ferrero-Waldner, B. (2005). *9th May Message from EU External Relations Commissioner Benita Ferrero-Waldner*, presented at the EU Delegation to the USA (Retrieved 05.11.2009, from www.eurunion.org/eu/index2.php?option=com_content&do_pdf=1&id=2375).

Ferrero-Waldner, B. (2006). *The EU in the World*, presented at the European Policy Centre Breakfast Briefing (Retrieved 11.10.2009, from www.europa.eu/rapid/pressReleasesAction.do?reference=SPEECH/06/59&format=HTML&aged=0&language=EN&guiLanguage=en).

Follath, E. and W. Wagner (22 June 1998). Der zweite Schock. *Der Spiegel*. Hamburg: Spiegel Redaktion.

Gilson, J. (2002). *Asia Meets Europe. Inter-regionalism and the Asia-Europe Meeting*. Cheltenham: Edward Elgar.

Gilson, J. (2004). Trade relations between Europe and East Asia. *Asia Europe Journal*, 2(2), pp. 185–200.

GIZ and ASEAN Secretariat (2009). *ASEAN-German Regional Forest Programme*. Jakarta: GIZ and ASEAN Secretariat.

Gorman, D. and T. Kivimäki (2008). *Non-Governmental Actors in Peace Processes: the Case of Aceh*. Geneva: Henry Dunant Centre for Humanitarian Dialogue.

Gunaratna, R. (2002). *Inside Al Qaeda: Global Network of Terror*. New York: Berkeley Books.

Gunaratna, R. (2006). *Terrorism in Southeast Asia: Threat and Response*, vol. 1. New York: Hudson Institute.

Bibliography

Hänggi, H. (2006). Interregionalism as a Multi-Faceted Phenomenon: in Search of a Typology. In H. Hänggi, R. Roloff and J. Rüland (eds.), *Interregionalism and International Relations*. New York: Routledge, pp. 31–62.

Higgott, R. (1998). Shared Response to the Market Shocks? *World Today*, 54(1), pp. 4–6.

High Representative and European Commission. (2008). *Climate Change and International Security*. Brussels: European Commission.

Hoadley, S. (2006). The Evolution of Security Thinking: an Overview. In S. Hoadley and J. Rüland (Eds.), *Asian Security Reassessed*. Singapore: Institute of Southeast Asian Studies, pp. 3–30.

Huxley, T. (1993). *Insecurity in the ASEAN Region*. London: The Royal United Services Institute for Defence Studies.

International Herald Tribune (23 January 2004). Avian Flu in Humans Spreads to Thailand (Retrieved 29.07.2009, from www.iht.com/articles/126281.html 4.10).

International Institute for Strategic Studies (2013). Speech by by the EU High Representative Catherine Ashton at the 12th Shangri-la Dialogue in 2013.

Interview with AMM official (10 February 2009).

Interview with ASEAN ISIS representative (31 October 2008).

Interview with ASEAN member state official (2 November 2008).

Interview with ASEAN member state official (21 November 2008).

Interview with ASEAN member state official (31 May 2010).

Interview with ASEAN Secretariat official (25 May 2010).

Interview with Asian think tank representative (10 November 2008).

Interview with the director of ILEA (3 December 2009).

Interview with EU member state official (24 May 2010).

Interview with EU official (6 February 2008).

Interview with EU official (4 November 2009).

Interview with EU official (5 February 2009).

Interview with EU official (9 February 2009).

Interview with EU official (18 November 2008).

Interview with EU official (19 November 2009).

Interview with EU official (27 May 2010).

Interview with European Commission official (15 February 2009).

Interview with European Commission official (16 February 2009).

Interview with European Commission official (20 February 2009).

Interview with former Commission official working for Wilhelm Haferkamp (15 February 2009).

Interview with GIZ staff (25 May 2010).

Interview with GIZ staff (26 May 2010).

Jamil, S. and B. Hersutanto (2007). *Workshop on Humanitarian Emergencies and Human Security: Lessons from Aceh*. Banda Aceh.

Jepperson, R. L., P. J. Katzenstein and A. Wendt (1996). Norms, Identity, and Culture in National Security. In P. J. Katzenstein (ed.), *The Culture of National*

Security: Norms and Identity in World Politics. New York: Columbia University Press, pp. 33–75.

Jetschke, A. (2009). Institutionalizing ASEAN: Celebrating Europe through Network Governance. *Cambridge Review of International Affairs*, 22(3), pp. 407–426.

Johnston, A. I. (1995a). *Cultural Realism: Strategic Culture and Grand Strategy in Chinese History*. Princeton University Press.

Johnston, A. I. (1995b). Thinking about Strategic Culture. *International Security*, 19(4), pp. 32–64.

Johnston, A. I. (1996). Cultural Realism and Strategy in Maoist China. In P. J. Katzenstein (ed.), *The Culture of National Security: Norms and Identity in World Politics*. New York: Columbia University Press, pp. 216–268.

Katzenstein, P. J. (2005). *A World of Regions. Asia and Europe in the American Imperium*. Ithaca: Cornell University Press.

Keohane, R. O. and J. S. Nye (1977). *Power and Interdependence: World Politics in Transition*. Boston: Little Brown and Company.

Kerr, W. A., N. Perdikis and M. T. Yeung (eds.). (1999). *Regional Trading Blocs in the Global Economy: the EU and ASEAN*. Cheltenham: Edward Elgar.

Kiatpongsarn, C. (2011). *The EU–Thailand Relations: Tracing the Patterns of New Bilateralism*. Amsterdam University Press.

Krasner, S. D. (1991). Global Communications and National Order: Life on the Pareto Frontier. *World Politics*, 43(3), pp. 336–366.

Kyodo News (28 January 2004). Global Collaboration Urged to Contain Bird Flu Epidemic, ProMED-mail (Retrieved 12.02.2010, from www.promedmail.org/pls/apex/f?p=2400:1202:3818374213884994::NO::F2400_P1202_CHECK_DISPLAY,F2400_P1202_PUB_MAIL_ID:X,24284).

Langhammer, R. (2001). The Face Value of ASEAN–EU Economic Cooperation after the Crisis: Is Cooperation Irrelevant, Impotent or Ineffective? In S. Chirathivat, F. Knipping, P. H. Lassen and C. S. Yue (eds.), *Asia-Europe on the Eve of the 21st Century*. Singapore: Institute for Southeast Asian Studies, pp. 103–132.

Lee, C. (ed.). (2000). *Asia-Europe Cooperation after the 1997–1998 Asian Turbulence*. Aldershot: Ashgate.

Lindley-French, J. (2005). The Revolution in Security Affairs: Hard and Soft Security Dynamics in the 21st Century. In A. Aldis and G. P. Herd (eds.), *Soft Security Threats and European Security*. London: Routledge, pp. 1–16.

Lipscy, P. (2003). Japan's Asian Monetary Fund Proposal. *Stanford Journal of East Asian Affairs*, 3(1), pp. 93–104.

MacDonald, A. and G. M. Viñals (2012). The EU and Mindanao: Innovative Avenues for Seeking Peace. *EUISS Occasional Paper* (97). Paris. EUISS.

McNeil, F. (2002). Security Implications of Asia's Environmental Problems. In M. G. Manwaring (ed.), *Environmental Security and Global Stability: Problems and Responses*. Lanham: Lexington Books, pp. 29–49.

Mahncke, D. (1997). European Interest and Southeast Asian Security. *Journal of European Studies*, 5(2), pp. 1–15.

Maier-Knapp, N. (2010). A Friend in Need. A Friend in Deed? ASEAN–EU Interregionalism in the Light of Non-Traditional Security Crises in South-East Asia. *Austrian Journal of Southeast Asian Studies*, 3(1), pp. 76–100.

Maier-Knapp, N. (2011a). Op-Ed: Europe and Asia – Working Together on Non-traditional Security Challenges (Retrieved 22.12.2011, from www.global-europe.org/detail-articles.php?articles=0000000007).

Maier-Knapp, N. (2011b). Regional and Interregional Integrative Dynamics of ASEAN and EU in Response to the Avian Influenza. *Asia Europe Journal*, 8(4), pp. 76–100.

Maier-Knapp, N. (2012). The EU and Non-Traditional Security in Southeast Asia. In C. Portela and D. Novotny, *EU–ASEAN Relations in the 21st Century: Strategic Partnership in the Making*. Basingstoke: Palgrave Macmillan, pp. 26–42.

Maier-Knapp, N. (2014). The European Union as a Normative Actor and its External Relations with Southeast Asia, *Journal of Contemporary European Research*. 10(2), pp. 221–235.

Manea, M.-G. (2008). Human rights and the Interregional Dialogue between Asia and Europe: ASEAN–EU Relations and ASEM. *The Pacific Review*, 21(3), pp. 369–396.

Manners, I. (2002). Normative Power Europe: a Contradiction in Terms? *Journal of Common Market Studies,* 40(2), pp. 235–258.

Martenczuk, B. (2004). Community Cooperation Policy and Conflict Prevention. In V. Kronenberger and J. Wouters (eds.), *The European Union and Conflict Prevention: Policy and legal Aspects*. Cambridge University Press, pp. 89–210.

May, B. (2000). Think Tanks in ASEAN-EU Relations: European Perspective. *Panorama*, 37–44 (Retrieved 09.10.2008, from www.dgap.org/publikationen/view/1f739a72cb0911da96bf6ba28e3f88078807.html).

Missiroli, A. (2008). Revisiting the European Security Strategy – Beyond 2008, *EPC Policy Brief* (Retrieved 26.05.2009, from www.epc.eu/TEWN/pdf/835822279_Revisiting%20the%20ESS.pdf).

Neumann, P. R. (2009). *Old and New Terrorism*. Cambridge: Polity Press.

Neves, M. S. (2004). *Changes in Southeast Asia and its Impact on EU-ASEAN Relations*. Lisbon: Institute of International and Strategic Studies.

Nguitragool, P. (2010), *Environmental Cooperation in Southeast Asia: ASEAN's Regime for Trans-Boundary Haze Pollution*. Abingdon: Routledge.

Nye Jr., J. S. (1990). *Bound to Lead: the Changing Nature of American Power*. New York: Basic Books.

Nye Jr., J. S. (2004). *Power in the Global Information Age*. London: Routledge.

Oye, K. A. (1986). Explaining Cooperation under Anarchy: Hypotheses and Strategies. In K. A. Oye (ed.), *Cooperation under Anarchy*. Princeton University Press, pp. 1–24.

Palmujoki, E. (2001). *Regionalism and Globalism in Southeast Asia*. Basingstoke: Palgrave Macmillan.

Patten, C. (2003). Together, Europe and Asia can make a difference. *Asia Europe Journal,* 1(4), pp. 481–482.

Peou, S. (2002). *Toward a Eurasian Security Community? The Case of ASEAN and EU.* Bangkok: Institute of Security and International Relations.

Petersson, M. (2006). Myanmar in EU–ASEAN Relations, *Asia Europe Journal* 4(4), pp. 563–581.

Pitsuwan, S. (1 June 1998). *Currency Turmoil in Southeast Asia: The Strategic Impact*, speech at the 12th Asia-Pacific Roundtable.

Pitsuwan, S. (12 June 1998). Opening Statement for the 31st ASEAN Ministerial Meeting and Post-Ministerial Meeting in Bangkok (Retrieved 01.07.2008, from www.asean.org/communities/asean-political-security-community/category/the-31st-ammpmc).

Presidency of the European Council (1998). *Cardiff European Council: presidency conclusions* (Retrieved 22.02.2009, from www.consilium.europa.eu/uedocs/cms_data/docs/pressdata/en/ec/54315.pdf).

Pushpanathan, S. (2003). *ASEAN Efforts to Combat Terrorism,* presented at the Second APEC Counter-Terrorism Task Force Meeting (Retrieved 13.05.2009, from www.aseansec.org/15060.htm).

Putnam, R. D. (1988). Diplomacy and Domestic Politics: the Logic of Two-Level Games. *International Organization,* 42(3), pp. 427–460.

Ravenhill, J. (2003). The New Bilateralism in the Asia Pacific. *Third World Quarterly,* 24(2), pp. 299–317.

Reuters (21 September 2005). WHO – Asia Must Change Age-Old Farming Practices to Stop Disease ProMED-mail.

Reuters AlertNet (11 October 2005). Bird Flu Delegation Tours Model Thai Farm, ProMED-mail.

Robles Jr., A. C. (2004). *The Political Economy of Interregional Relations: ASEAN and the EU.* Aldershot: Ashgate.

Robles Jr., A. C. (2008). *The Asia-Europe Meeting: the Theory and Practice of Interregionalism.* Abingdon: Routledge.

Roy, A. K. (2009). Addressing Pandemic Preparedness in ASEAN: the Ways Forward. In M. Caballero Anthony (ed.), *RSIS Monograph: Pandemic Preparedness in Asia.* Singapore: S. Rajaratnam School of International Studies, 16, pp. 128–132.

Rüland, J. (2002a). The European Union as an Inter- and Transregional Actor: Lessons for Global Governance from Europe's Relations with Asia. *National Europe Centre Paper,* 13 (Retrieved 04.11.2007, from www.digitalcollections.anu.edu.au/bitstream/1885/41658/3/ruland.pdf).

Ruland, J. (2002b). Inter- and Transregionalism: Remarks on the State of the Art of a New Research Agenda. *National Europe Centre Paper,* 35 (Retrieved 04.11.2007, from www.anu.edu.au/NEC/Archive/ruland2.pdf).

Rüland, J. (2002c). *Interregionalism in International Relations: Conference Summary,* presented at the Interregionalism in International Relations Conference in Freiburg.

Rüland, J. (2005). The Nature of Southeast Asian Security Challenges. *Security Dialogue,* 36(4), pp. 545–563.

Sastry, Narayan (2002). Forest Fires, Air Pollution and Mortality in Southeast Asia, *Demography*, 39(1), pp. 1–23.

Schmitter, P. (1970). A Revised Theory of Regional Integration. *International Organisation*, 24(4): 836–868.

Schulze, K. E. (2007). Mission Not So Impossible. The Aceh Monitoring Mission and Lessons Learned for the EU. *International Policy Analysis* (Retrieved 12.12.2008, from www.library.fes.de/pdf-files/id/04786.pdf).

Segal, G. and D.-I. Shin (1997). Getting Serious about Asia–Europe Security Cooperation, *Survival*, 39(1), pp. 138–155.

Selth, A. (2008). Even Paranoids Have Enemies: Cyclone Nargis and Myanmar's Fear of Invasion. *Contemporary Southeast Asia*, 30(3), pp. 379–402.

Siemens, A. (14 November 2008). Der schräge Mythos eines Kaffs. *Focus* (Retrieved 12.01.2011, from www.focus.de/finanzen/boerse/finanzkrise/weltfinanzgipfel-der-schraege-mythos-eines-kaffs_aid_348484.html).

Sjöstedt, G. (1977). *The External Role of the European Community*. Farnborough: Saxon House.

Smith, K. E. (2005). Still 'Civilian Power EU'?. *European Foreign Policy Unit*, 1–19 (Retrieved 15.06.2008, from www.lse.ac.uk/Depts/intrel/pdfs/EFPU%20Working%20Paper%202005-1.pdf).

Sukma, R. (2004). *Security Operations in Aceh: goals, consequences and lessons*. Washington DC: East-West Centre.

The Guardian (2007). The 2004 Madrid bombings (Retrieved 22.01.2010, from www.guardian.co.uk/world/2007/oct/31/spain.menezes).

The Nation (20 January 2004). Bird Flu Not Here: EU Commissioner.

Timmer, D. (2000). Livelihood Security and Forests. *Arbour Vitae*, 16.

Tow, W. (2004). Alternative Security Models: Implications for ASEAN. In E. Newman and R. Thakur (eds.), *Broadening Asia's Security Discourse and Agenda: Political, Social, and Environmental Perspectives*. New York: UN University Press, pp. 245–269.

Umbach, F. (2004). EU–ASEAN Political and Security Dialogue at the Beginning of the 21st Century: Prospects for Interregional Cooperation on International Terrorism. In C. Dürkop (ed.), *Panorama: Insights into Southeast Asian and European Affairs*. Singapore: Konrad-Adenauer Stiftung, pp. 9–22.

UN News Centre (2008). Global Food Crisis 'Silent Tsunami' Threatening Over 100 Million People, Warns UN.

Söderbaum, F. and L. van Langenhove (2006). Introduction: the EU as a Global Actor and the Role of Interregionalism. In F. Söderbaum and L. van Langenhove (eds.), *The EU as a Global Player. The Politics of Interregionalism*. London: Routledge, pp. 1–14.

Söderbaum, F., P. Stalgren and L. van Langenhove (2006). The EU as a Global Actor and the Dynamics of Interregionalism: a Comparative Analysis. In F. Söderbaum and L. van Langenhove (eds.), *The EU as a Global Player. The Politics of Interregionalism*. London: Routledge, pp. 117–132.

Wahlström, M. (11 January 2012). *Securing Our Common Future: Strengthening the Resilience of Communities and Nations*, address to the Summit on Resilience, Pace University, New York.

Waldman, P. (1 October 1997). Southeast Asia Smog Is Tied to Politics, *The Wallstreet Journal Europe*.

Wiener, A. (2008). European Responses to International Terrorism: Diversity Awareness as a New Capability? *Journal of Common Market Studies,* 46(1), pp. 195–218.

World Bank (2003). *Asian Financial Crisis Response Fund 1: Completion Report.* Washington DC: ASEM.

Wurzel, R. K. W. (2008). Environmental Policy: EU Actors, Leader and Laggard States. In J. Hayward (ed.), *Leaderless Europe*. Oxford University Press, pp. 66–88.

Xinhua News Agency (via COMTEX) (18 August 2002). Thailand: More Than 68 000 People Infected with Dengue Fever Virus (Retrieved 12.11.2010, from www.promedmail.org/pls/apex/f?p=2400:1202:3818374213884994::NO::F2400_P1202_CHECK_DISPLAY,F2400_P1202_PUB_MAIL_ID:X,19109).

Yeo, L. H. (2009). The EU as a Security Actor in Southeast Asia. *Security Politics in Asia and Europe*. In W. Hofmeister (ed.), Singapore: Konrad Adenauer Stiftung, pp. 9–24.

Youngs, R. (2008). Fusing Security and Development: Just Another Europlatitude? *Journal of European Integration,* 30(3), pp. 419–437.

Zartman, W. I. (2008). *Negotiation and Conflict Management: Essays on Theory and Practice*. New York: Routledge.

Index

Aceh xv, xvi, 1–2, 10, 78, 86–100, 110, 116
Aceh Monitoring Mission (AMM) 2, 23, 84, 86–98, 100–18
actor 3–6, 9–11, 14–15, 22–3, 41, 47–8, 55, 59–64, 66, 70, 73, 79–83, 88, 92–9, 102–3, 105–10, 113–17, 119, 121, 122, 124, 125; -centric 3, 15; international 3, 5, 8, 13, 20, 41, 45, 55, 62–3, 98, 106, 109–10, 115, 120, 123–4; non-state 20, 30, 55, 59, 60–2, 64, 81, 85, 98, 107, 108, 120; NTS 9, 82, 97, 109, 120, 121, 122; political 2, 40, 115; politico-security 2, 7, 8, 11, 107–9, 121; by proxy 109; state-affiliated 60, 64, 109
adaptive capacity 3
Asian Financial Crisis (AFC) 5–6, 8, 10, 32–9, 41, 45–7, 49–52, 54, 58, 62, 64, 87, 101, 110
ASEAN Plus Three (APT) 32, 33, 101
ASEAN Regional Forum (ARF) 22, 24, 45–7, 67, 75–6, 80–1, 108
ASEAN Secretariat 22, 24, 37, 49, 61, 76, 101, 105, 109, 112, 113, 116
ASEAN Way 19, 55
ASEAN–EU: dialogue 3, 6, 11, 19–20, 41, 45–6, 49, 67, 69, 73, 81, 101, 122; interaction 123; Migration and Border Management Programme 74; relationship 3, 6–7, 9, 14–15, 17, 19, 20, 24, 30, 38, 40, 47, 54, 58–9, 80, 108, 115, 117, 119–22
Asia–Europe Foundation (ASEF) 74
Asia–Europe Meeting (ASEM) 19, 24, 36, 38, 39–45, 48, 50, 67, 73–5, 80–1, 104, 108, 121; Bond Fund 42; FinMM xvi, 41–5; YES xvii, 42
assistance: and cooperation 45; development 63–4, 75, 93–4, 121; financial 23, 27–9, 33, 35–6, 41, 45–7, 79, 98–9, 103, 105; and the haze 55–9, 61; humanitarian 1, 9, 20, 28, 105, 106–7; security 23, 66, 69
avian influenza 10, 66–83, 101, 104, 110, 115

Bali bombings 10, 28, 66–76, 82–3, 110, 118
Boxing Day Tsunami 1–2, 4, 6, 28, 77, 111

capabilities 25–6, 31, 54, 95–6, 115–16, 118, 123
capacity-building 27–8, 30, 56–7, 91, 104
cartoon controversy 72
catalysts: and ASEAN 17; and cooperative dynamics 4; and European norms/standards 81, 119; and regional integration 37; and the role of the ARF 46
Catherine Ashton 7, 24, 25, 119
ceasefires 86–8
Chiang Mai Initiative 32
China 16–17, 37–8, 41, 50, 125
civilians 25, 30, 87, 92, 95, 97, 103, 105–6, 108
climate change 7, 44, 62, 102
'commonalisation' 119, 123
Common Security and Defence Policy (CSDP) 10, 24–8, 30, 82, 88, 90–5, 99, 104, 108–10, 116
Communism/-ist 16–7, 21, 99
constructivism 14
contagion 34–5, 41, 78, 110
cooperation i, 3–5, 7–12, 14–16, 18–24, 29–31, 33–5, 39, 42–7, 50, 54–61, 64, 66, 68–74, 78–81, 86, 89, 94–6, 98, 100–2, 104–5, 107, 111, 113–17, 119–22, 125; regional cooperation 5, 20, 54, 78, 80, 100

Index

cost-benefit calculations 35–6, 108–9, 111, 120
counter-terrorism xvii, 44, 66, 70, 71–5, 82, 115
Crisis Management Initiative (CMI) 67, 87
crisis i, xv, xvi, 4–6, 9, 11, 12, 22, 24, 26–8, 32–50, 56, 58, 64, 73, 78–9, 81, 87, 89, 91–2, 94–8, 100–5, 108–13, 120, 122, 125; -centric i, 3, 5–6, 9

Danes 72–3
Denmark 58, 72–3, 76
development 3–4, 9, 14–19, 21, 24–31, 35, 37–8, 42, 45, 50, 52, 54–7, 60–1, 63–4, 66, 70, 73, 75, 77, 79–82, 84, 93, 96–7, 101–2, 105–8, 112, 116–17, 119–23
Development Cooperation Instrument (DCI) 29–30
Directorate General for External Relations (DG RELEX) 79, 89
disaster 1–2, 5, 10–11, 24, 26, 28–9, 42, 98, 103, 105, 108, 123
Disaster Preparedness ECHO (DIPECHO) 28–9

energy security 101–2, 117
European Commission xiv, xv, 1–2, 5–6, 15–16, 19–20, 23–4, 26–31, 34, 38–9, 42–4, 46, 48, 55–64, 69–73, 79, 82, 84, 87, 89–94, 97–9, 101, 103, 106–8, 110, 113, 115, 122, 124
European Commission's Humanitarian Aid Office (ECHO) 1, 20, 28–30, 34
European Community (EC) 15–17
European Council 20, 25–6, 28, 30, 35, 69, 74, 78, 83, 88–93, 101–2
European External Action Service (EEAS) 11, 123–4
European Financial Expertise Network (EFEX) 36, 38–9
eurozone i, 5, 6, 12, 105, 108, 113, 120
extremism 7, 24, 74, 76

fire 53, 56, 57, 58, 59, 61
food security 10, 30, 101, 102
Forest Law Enforcement, Governance and Trade (FLEGT) 58
forest xvi, 2, 31, 51–3, 56–9, 61–4, 101–2
Free Aceh Movement (GAM) 85–8, 90–1, 93, 96, 99, 113

Germany 34–5, 54, 61, 68, 75, 78
globalisation 29, 52, 63

Index 139

governance 20, 22, 42, 52, 58, 61–2, 69, 80, 93, 97, 102, 106, 113–4
Government of Indonesia (GoI) 52, 84–5, 87–8, 93, 95–6

haze xvi, 10, 29, 51–65, 110, 125
hegemony/hegemonic 8, 62, 120, 122–5
human/-ism 8, 32, 52, 60, 64, 79, 81, 87, 96, 104, 106, 125; -centred 4; -oriented 9; rights 16–18, 20, 23, 70, 74, 76, 84, 89, 92–3, 95, 96, 98–9, 105, 106, 109–11, 118; security 9, 96, 111
humanitarian 1–2, 9, 14, 18, 20, 24, 28, 30, 76, 90, 96, 98, 103, 105–9, 117, 121–3

Indochina 16–7
Indonesia 1, 2, 18, 22, 28, 34, 35, 37–8, 51–61, 63–4, 66, 69, 70, 72, 77, 83–8, 91–4, 100, 110, 125
insecurity 10, 13, 20, 27, 42, 49, 75, 82, 95, 100, 111, 122–3
institutional issues i, xiv, 4–5, 8, 15, 25–6, 32, 39–40, 46, 52, 79, 82, 89–90, 94, 97, 100, 112–15, 117, 124
Instrument for Stability (IfS) 26–8, 30, 105–7
integrative dynamic i, 4, 10, 11, 13, 37, 51, 52, 55, 66, 82, 125
International Law Enforcement Academy (ILEA) 71–3
International Monetary Fund (IMF) 33–6, 40–3, 47, 50
inter-regional/-ism i, 3–4, 6–9, 11–13, 15, 24, 30–1, 39–40, 42, 49–50, 58, 64, 67, 73–4, 79–80, 94, 108, 111–17, 122–3
Investment Promotion Action Plan (IPAP) 39

Jakarta Centre of Law Enforcement Co-operation (JCLEC) 71, 72
Javier Solana 83, 89–90, 116
Jemaah Islamiah (JI) xvi, 66, 83, 86
Jörn Dosch xiv, 7, 8, 19, 26, 105
Jürgen Rüland 3, 8, 15, 23, 65, 114

Laos 77, 79, 101–2
Law on the Governance of Aceh (LoGA) 93
liberal-democratic agenda 4, 107, 111, 117, 119; and identity 123

maritime security 5, 10, 22, 24, 86
Martti Ahtisaari 87–8, 90, 93
Memorandum of Understanding (MoU) 87–9, 93, 96, 99

140 Index

military 8, 11, 13–4, 19–20, 22–6, 30, 62, 67, 76, 80, 83, 85, 86–8, 91, 94, 97, 98–9, 102–3, 105–6, 122; might 8; strength 8, 26
Millennium Development Goal (MDG) 29, 102
Mindanao 94, 105–6
Myanmar 5–6, 14, 18–20, 41, 45–6, 59, 83, 100, 102–4, 107, 125

Nargis 20, 100, 102–3
national sovereignty 5, 16, 26, 33, 58, 112
NATO 25, 109
New Asia Strategy 18
A New Partnership for Southeast Asia 23
non-governmental organization (NGO) 1, 93, 105–6, 108–9
non-interference 5, 18, 32–3, 94, 97, 109–10
non-proliferation 5, 7, 22, 28, 105
non-traditional security (NTS) 4, 9, 10, 11–12, 14–15, 17, 20–6, 30–1, 49, 55, 60–2, 64–5, 76, 80, 82–3, 97–100, 102, 109, 111, 115–25; actor 9, 82, 97, 120–2; crisis/-es 3, 10, 11–18, 15, 23, 60, 77, 87, 109, 113, 115, 120–1, 124
normative agenda 5, 14–5, 23, 33, 40, 43–4, 49, 59–60, 62, 64, 66, 81, 97–8, 104–5, 107–8, 109, 111–14, 116–20, 123, 124; actor 28, 83, 107, 110–14, 116–17, 120, 124; and context 14; and dilemmas 20; and identity/-ies 14, 20, 23, 60, 74, 96, 110, 120, 124; and influence 14, 23, 93, 107, 113, 120, 124
Nuremberg Declaration 2, 22, 94

Organisation for Security Cooperation in Europe (OSCE) 8, 75–6, 109
othering 107, 119, 123, 125
outbreak: of the Asian Financial Crisis 34; of avian influenza 10, 77–9, 81–2, 101, 104, 110

peace process 87–8, 91, 93, 97, 105
perceptions 5, 10, 13–5, 17, 23, 35, 47, 58–9, 62, 67, 72, 76, 78, 81–3, 110, 119, 121–2
Philippines 28, 37–8, 52, 69, 71, 78, 83, 100, 105
politicisation 10, 14, 29, 31, 56, 119
politico-security i, 6–9, 11, 15–7, 20–1, 24, 98, 106–9, 121–2, 124
preventive diplomacy 75–6, 90

Rapid Reaction Mechanism (RRM) 1, 26–8, 70–1, 89, 108, 110

regional dynamics i, xi, 6, 10, 13, 15, 37; 51–2, 54–5, 66, 125; and integration 4-7, 10, 30, 33, 37, 40, 43, 49, 50, 54, 64, 66, 79, 112
Regional EU–ASEAN Dialogue Instrument (READI) 21, 101
rhetoric 19, 24, 40, 45, 60, 74, 93, 97, 99, 103, 111, 116, 118, 120–1
risk 11, 14, 23, 28–9, 32, 51, 69, 75, 77, 82, 107, 113–14, 119–23

security: capability/-ies 28; community 17; -development 14, 27, 30, 82, 121; dimension 7, 17; interest 26; assistance 23, 66, 69
September 11 attacks 6, 12, 66–9, 72, 75, 82, 86
Shangri-La Dialogue 7, 24, 117
social action theory 14–5
socio-economic politics 28, 36, 52, 62, 64, 66, 82, 100, 116–17, 119
sociological 'other' 109
Southeast Asia Regional Centre for Counter Terrorism (SEARCCT) 72
strategy/-em 78, 80, 89, 94, 97–8, 101, 108, 111, 117–19, 121, 123
supranational 30, 63, 76, 82, 109, 111, 113, 115, 118, 124–5
swine flu 104

technocratisation 60–1
terrorism/-ist xvii, 6, 7, 12, 21–4, 44, 66–76, 82, 83, 85–6, 99, 111, 115, 122
Thailand 6, 34, 37–8, 52, 69, 71, 77, 79, 81, 83, 86, 94, 100–1, 103, 106
threat construction 13, 78, 108, 110, 117
timber 51, 53, 64
Trade Facilitation Action Plan (TFAP) 39
transboundary challenges 2, 5, 7, 10, 24, 51, 54–5, 61, 64, 107
Trans-Regional EU–ASEAN Trade Initative (TREATI) 21
turmoil 6, 33

United Nations (UN) 23, 58, 69–70, 74, 79, 87–8, 93, 96, 100–3, 105
United States of America (USA) 47–9, 55, 66, 67, 71, 73, 76, 78, 83, 86, 88, 94, 116

Vietnam 17, 28, 37–8, 77–9, 100
violence 85, 100, 106, 110
vulnerability/ies 5, 27, 29, 40, 49, 51, 119, 122